Seen and Not Heard

SCOTTISH CHILDREN
1844 ~ 1944

Sheila Livingstone

HAMILTON

SCOTTISH LIBRARY ASSOCIATION

1998

Contents

For
Amber, Marc and Siobhan

**Scottish Library
Association**

Scottish Centre for Information
& Library Services
1 John Street
Hamilton ML3 7EU

© Sheila Livingstone 1998
ISBN 0 90064 49 6

Designed by GSB, Edinburgh.

Printed by Portobello Printers
Midlothian

Introduction

Children who were seen and not heard have always been considered the ideal in Scotland. Speak when you are spoken to! Don't interrupt! Never be pushy and never show-off. These were the instructions given by parents. This has led to the almost impossible task of tracking down information about individual children. Much is written about the adults who took on responsibility for their education, welfare and behaviour but there is a dearth of material giving the children's point of view.

The period covered in this book is from the 1840s -1940s. This was chosen as being a time of progress when it was beginning to be realised that children had different needs from adults. These needs were addressed by men and women of forethought and action, many of them driven by their Christian faith into saving the souls of the children of the damned, as they saw it. It is from this philanthropic era that many of the Scottish child care institutions date and governments began to legislate for children in employment and at risk from neglect.

Many of their ideas may today seem authoritarian and even ill-advised. They did not provide a life of cushioned ease but there were attempts to deal with major problems. Children had no rights, were open to exploitation and in many ways were seen as expendable.

The topics discussed are education, work, health, welfare, wartime, crime and social and home life is touched upon. The ironic fact which surfaces in education is that most of what are now considered the most exclusive schools started out as institutions for those who had become impoverished or were too poor to afford to pay for an education.

Children are no longer permitted to work the long hours and in the miserable conditions which many of them endured during the heyday of the Industrial Revolution. The exploitation by parents and employers was horrendous.

Many children died in infancy or childhood. Health and welfare services were mainly provided by charities and those who were handicapped were treated like second class citizens. Many children were driven to a life of crime yet we must not forget that there were privileged children who did live a comfortable life with servants, governesses, ponies and the latest toys but they were in the minority. Research into the lives of Scottish children is piecemeal and an area ripe for further development.

Sheila Livingstone

Home and Social Life

East Dunbartonshire Libraries.

The home and social life of children differed greatly depending on the class status of their family. The Victorians were extremely class conscious. The upper-class and the upper middle-class treated their children as ornaments. They dressed both boys and girls under two years of age in frills. Those a little older were dressed like cut-down adults in velvet and lace, fur in winter and layers of underclothing. Little boys sported sailor suits and wore the kilt on Sundays. They delighted in having them photographed when this medium first appeared and before that they had portraits of their children painted by an artist.

Dress

Clothes were divided into Sunday best, Saturday and everyday. All 'respectable' families tried to keep some clothes for special to wear to attend the church on Sundays. New bonnets were needed at Easter and New Year.

In Edwardian times, at the beginning of the twentieth century, little had changed in the way in which fashionable children were dressed but by 1910 more colour appeared and white was popular, even with boys. They often sported knickerbockers, blazers and straw hats, like cut down versions of their elders.

Many children envied those who did not have to wear shoes in summer. Neil Barry complains:

My mother will never let me have my feet bare in the summer, even when almost all the boys and girls in Heather Street go without shoes.

Mrs Barry, Frederick Niven, 1933

As late as World War Two few children would be allowed to visit the 'town', as the nearest city was called, unless they were dressed in their best coat, hat and gloves. These were often fawn covert coats - a fine material like that of which suits are often made, usually with a stitched velvet Peter Pan collar. Boys wore caps and girls felt round hats with an elastic beneath the chin, in winter, and straw bonnets decorated with little rosebuds in summer. White

gloves, short white socks and leather shoes with a crossover strap which was fastened with a button completed the outfit for girls while boys wore three-quarter length stockings and boots.

Other less well off children, if they were not barefooted, wore Wellingtons even in summer. Their clothes were patched and were often too big or too small. Shoes and boots were down at heel and let in water and cuffs and collars were frayed at the edges. Elbows of sweaters and jackets were patched. Some children had their chests wrapped in brown paper and were sewn into their underwear for the winter. Hygiene was not a strong point. It was much easier to tell the social standing of a child from their dress up until 1944 than in the years which followed.

The majority of children wore hand knitted garments and often also home sewn clothes. These were sometimes made from clothing which had belonged to an adult and was recut to fit a child. Pinafores were popular for girls because they gave protection to their dresses and blouses. Liberty bodices with rubber buttons were worn to keep warm.

Up until the 1950s most boys wore short trousers till they had left school and started working. At school girls wore gymslips, tied with a sash, ankle socks in summer, up until fifth year, and lisle stockings or three quarter length socks in winter.

Boots were the common footwear for boys and girls up until 1908 when shoes began to appear. Boys liked tackety boots for sliding on frosty days.

Babies were swaddled in layers of clothes to keep them warm. They were christened in beautiful cotton and muslin robes decorated with

Ayrshire embroidery. Well-off families had nannies or nursemaids who wheeled their charges around the park in elegant perambulators, the proper name for a pram. Designs changed over the years and folding prams appeared which had a section which allowed older children to sit.

Home life

Few houses had baths or hot water systems. Baths were taken in the kitchen in front of the fire in a tin or zinc bath which was kept beneath the bed and brought out to be filled with hot water, heated on a stove or range. Some children in towns would visit the public baths. Many children slept on pull-out beds which were stored away during the day and they often had to share their bed with their brothers and sisters. Few houses had indoor toilets and these were either in the back garden or on a stair landing and were shared by several families.

Sundays

In the latter half of the nineteenth century children were brought up strictly, especially where religion was concerned. Every family had psalms, Bible reading and prayers twice a day. The children were catechised - which was a set of questions about the nature of God to which they had to know the answers and repeat them. The elders of the Church of Scotland could come round either at school or at home and examine them on their knowledge of the catechism.

Sundays, up until a decade after the Second World War, were strictly observed. Shops were closed, no washing was hung outside and attendance at church or Sunday school plus family visits filled the day. In the 1880s not even the fountains were allowed to be switched on. Children visiting relatives were expected to amuse themselves by looking out of the window, reading a book or playing a suitable board game. Looking through the family photograph album, or in some houses at 3D stereoscopes usually with photographs of climbers in the Alps, was a pastime which

children were allowed. Hymns or sacred tunes might be played on the piano or colouring in or painting Bible texts might be permitted. In the evening, in summer, the family might take a walk in the park or by the sea.

My first attendance at church [in the 1880s] *was made in her charge* [his grandmother]. *It was a United Presbyterian church, and there was a plate in the vestibule...On this occasion, the plate was very nearly my undoing. Misunderstanding my grandmother's gesture, and clean forgetting the penny in my glove, I was about to help myself liberally, when deeply affronted... she seized my hand and drew me indoors. Unwittingly I had saved a penny.*

I Remember, J. J. Bell, 1932

Radio

By the 1930s radios were common in homes. Children had their own programmes and Children's Hour, in the afternoon, was popular. Kathleen Garscadden was known as Auntie Kathleen and Willie McCulloch as Uncle Mac. Serials such as *Down at the Farm* were popular and Lavinia Derwent's *Tammy Troot* was also a favourite.

On Saturday night, during the war, I was dressed ready for bed and was allowed to stay up to hear 'Saturday Night Theatre', which performed well known dramatic plays such as J.M. Barrie's 'Mary Rose'. On Sundays it was Albert Sandler and his orchestra in 'Grand Hotel' and the scary 'The Man in Black' or Paul Temple mystery and detective stories. Radio made you use your imagination and when years later Paul Temple came on television he didn't look right.

Interview with Sheila Peters, 1997

Evenings might also be spent doing homework then as a treat playing a game of tiddely-winks, Happy Families, Old Maid or very young children might listen to nursery

rhyme records on a wind up gramophone for which the needles had to be changed after each record was played. There was a sense of community within the closes and if someone was baking they would share what they had made with all the children.

Mrs. McNeil she was great at making doughnuts. She got all the bairns up in her house... Kilmun Street was a sociable place - we weren't neighbours, we were friends. On a Saturday night when the children were in bed, the fathers and mothers would be out in the street dancing till two and three in the morning. I was the oldest girl among six brothers and five sisters. I once did a Highland fling at a dance when I was ten or eleven, there were melodeons and fiddlers.

Kilmun Street Before the War, Mrs. Rickart, oral history tape, 1990

Spunky Duncan's pet shop, Dundee, 1916.

Pets

Dogs, horses, pigeons, cats and even lambs were favourite pets. In Dundee, at the beginning of the twentieth century, Spunky Duncan did a roaring trade in whippets, pigeons and song birds. Boys and girls sometimes made a penny or two from feeding 'doos', as racing pigeons were called, when their owner was serving during World War One.

Fun outside

Children had little organised entertainment unless a visit to a pantomime or latterly a cinema. They made their own fun, often out-of-doors. Frost was always welcomed as was snow. Boys and girls had great fun when there was ice on the ground playing at 'keepin' the puddin' het'. Great speeds could be reached especially if wearing tackety-boots, or sitting on three-legged stools turned upside down. Tin trays were also a popular choice of vehicle. Wooden sledges with metal runners were often home made.

Boys following watercart, Coatbridge, 1910.

Wooden stilts provided a challenge and iron girds and cleeks were spun along for hours. Pavements provided a playground for chalked peever beds, the spinning of peeries, skipping ropes, single and double - many a girl was thrashed for pinching the washing line - bools or marbles and football. Balls were stotted against walls to appropriate actions and chants.

Every boy had to have a bogey, a wooden cart, home-made from a crate to which wheels and ropes were attached. These would be raced with fierce competition. There were also hundreds of singing, chasing and hide-and-seek type games which any number of players could join in.

Girls enjoyed collecting and swapping scraps. These were colourful cut-outs of fairies, nursery rhyme characters, flowers, etc. Some girls had scraps handed down from their family. These were known as pre-war (before 1939) and were made of thicker, glossier paper. These were coveted. Cut-out dolls, which were cardboard figures with a large wardrobe of clothes were another popular pastime. These were

especially prized if they came from the United States of America as they were often based on famous film stars.

Toys

Play in a mainly Presbyterian society was seen as sinful and a waste of time. From this stemmed the idea that toys could be permitted as long as they were in some way educational or morally improving. Middle-class parents began to provide toys such as wooden alphabet blocks for their children in the late nineteenth century.

Many wooden toys were hand-made. Rocking horses appeared in the best nurseries, small wooden dolls, Noah's Arks, train sets, building blocks, barrows, hobby-horses and cradles were prized and handed down through the generations. Tin toys began to appear followed by mechanical, wind-up toys. In the 1930s pedal cars, tricycles and bicycles were popular. Bisque and china dolls elaborately dressed were pushed around in wicker prams, later

Pram, tricycle and wooden blocks.

in metal bodied ones, and dolls' houses with miniature furniture appeared. Metal soldiers painted in regimental colours and Dinky cars and lorries were a boy's dream.

Back courts

Tenements provided backyard entertainment. Jeely-pieces - bread spread with jam - were thrown down from an open window. The more fussy mothers put them in a paper

bag. There were wash-houses and middens with roofs to play on. Concerts were organised and all the children 'did a turn'. Sometimes a one-man band would arrive, or a dancing bear or a barrel-organ complete with monkey. Children would be allowed to watch out of the window and then throw down a penny. The ragman went round collecting old clothes and offered a balloon in exchange.

Country ploys

Children who lived in the country could go rabbit hunting or fishing in the burns. They collected birds eggs, guddled for trout, made swings by tying a rope to a tree branch, went fox hunting, climbed hills and had all the freedom denied the town child. If they lived near the sea or by a loch they could go out in a rowing boat to fish, swim and dive.

Tricks

Boys throughout both centuries seemed to enjoy playing tricks, especially on grumpy folk who annoyed them. They pinned notices on their backs saying 'Kick Me!' or tied their door handles together and then rang the doorbell; buttons were tied by a thread and stuck to the window where they made a noise when pulled. Dead cats were put down chimneys, divots of peat put over chimneys to make the fire blow back and fill the room with smoke and hollow stems were dried and used to blow smoke through the keyholes of doors. These acts were often done for a dare, the object being not to be caught.

Free hurls on tramcars, carts and later lorries were a great attraction for boys. They would grab the pole at the open entrance to the tram but had to be quick to let go if the conductor appeared. The tail gates of carts and lorries served the same purpose. Following the water cart with bare feet and splashing around in its wake was fun but opening water hydrants to play in the ensuing fountain was not looked on kindly.

Sometimes boys could be cruel to those mentally handicapped - often described as 'not the full shilling'. In Biggar Daft Jock was employed in the brewery and the boys teased him by encouraging him to tumble, dance and sing which he did willingly. They also made him give them cuddy-rides by carrying them on his back. At Kirkintilloch Petticoat Dan was the butt of jokes. One boy met him carrying a can of milk and told him it was 'rinnin' oot'. Dan turned it upside down to see if it had a hole in it and then was amazed that the can was empty when the bottom was sound.

High days and holidays

Fairs

Many towns held several fairs each year. Everyone would dress in their best clothes and set out to enjoy the fun.

For months before frequent deposits were being made in our Penny Savings Bank, and when at last the anxiously expected morning arrived, with what feelings of pride did we make a 'run' upon the bank...of the accumulated coppers, not satisfied until [they] were transferred to the pockets of our new moleskins, donned for the first time in honour of 'The Moss'...to be soon spent at the Lucky Poke, lost at Wheel of Fortune...or taken from us at the Rowley Powley [a game of skittles].

Epilogue to the Old Vale and its Memories,
J. Ferguson and J. G. Temple, 1929

There were Punch and Judy stalls, sweetie stalls selling Coulter's candy, black-striped balls, gingerbread men and other goodies. Children were given fairings - peeries, dolls, ribbons, marbles or some other small gift. There were also swing-boats, round-a-bouts and coconut shys.

Annual outing, Gartferry 1938.   East Dunbartonshire Libraries.

Circuses

Hengler's Circus came to town with clowns and acrobats, bare back riders and spectacular scenery. Commercial interests were quick to jump on the publicity waggon even in 1900 when the Carnival in Glasgow staged 'Spectaculars' -

New Year

In Scotland, until after World War Two, Christmas was not as popular a festival as New Year. On Hogmanay, which was also called Cake Night, children went out guising as they still do at Hallowe'en.

*Ma feet's cauld
Ma shoon's thin;
Gie's ma cakes
An' let me rin.*

Traditional

On New Year's Day children opened their presents, while some still kept the old new year and waited until the twelfth of January. On New Year's Day outdoor sports were held: shinty, foot races, skating if the weather permitted and hand ball matches.

Outings

Many children never had a proper holiday in the sense of leaving home to sleep elsewhere overnight unless with relatives. Most children did have treats and outings which they valued. They were often taken on a Sunday to a nearby park or pleasant country area, or if they lived close to the seaside they visited the nearest resort. Sunday Schools, missions, societies and works had annual outings and picnics and there were many public celebrations also.

The Grassmarket Mission Outing

In Edinburgh the Grassmarket Mission Outing was held annually from 1886. In the 1920s, Councillor Alexander Barrie organised it and children sang this jingle:

> *I'm no goin' on Barrie's trip*
> *I'm no goin' again*
> *I'm no goin' on Barrie's trip*
> *It always comes on rain*
>
> Traditional

Up to 2,000 children would take part, marching to the tramcars which took them to Gorgie where every child was given a hot pie, a mug of tea and a bag of buns. People turned out to watch the procession and collectors took up offerings from them for the Mission fund.

Renfrew Poor Children's Excursion

The sixth Annual Outing took place in 1900. The children's parade in July set out, led by the Parkhead Reformatory Band to board a steamer to go 'Doon the Watter', as sailing down the River Clyde to the Firth of Clyde was known. Men from the shipyards cheered as the steamer passed along. People called out, 'It's the Poor's trip,' and waved from the shore. There were two categories of ticket: white entitled the owner to a poke - a paper bag - of goodies to eat while red tickets indicated those who had paid for their ticket and who brought their own picnic hampers.

Private benefactors

Many landowners entertained the local children once or twice a year. They would invite them into their estate for a picnic.

> *In autumn each year, members of the Sabbath Schools in connection with Maryhill Parish Church... were invited to Garscube by Sir George and Lady Campbell. The children assembled at the Parish Church early on a Saturday afternoon, with their respective teachers...the boys bearing a*

considerable display of flags, and headed generally by a fife and drum band, all marched off - Bob Miller, the beadle, following with an enormous bundle of tinned jugs slung over his shoulders for the distribution of tea or milk amongst the children, many of whom carried jugs of their own.

> Maryhill, 1750-1894,
> Alexander Thomson, 1895

Public ceremonies

The opening of a park or the laying of a foundation stone of a public building was often marked by a civic ceremony. When Clydebank Burgh Hall foundation stone was laid the children had their own celebration:

> ***Are ye gaun tae the trate?***
> *Milk boys and girls shouted this to each other on the morning of the 23rd June 1900. They assembled at 10.30am in the playground of their school wearing their best clothes and with a tinnie hanging on a ribbon round their necks. The boys wore jerseys and trousers with white rubber-collared shirts and the girls light coloured pinafores and blouses. Parents lined the route to watch as the infants in front, followed by each class in turn led by their teacher they followed a pipe band to a field in the east end of the town, Mr Fulton, the High School headmaster in charge. Carts pulled by the Co-op's best horses, gorgeous with flags and laden with baskets of pastries arrived, a gift from the Clydebank Co-operative Society who also supplied milk to drink. There were races, tumbling and tig for the 4000 children present. There was a singsong then they all marched back to their schools. "The best thing ever done in this dull, dirty Clydebank has been well done" was one comment.*

> *Clydebank Press*, June, 1900

Hospital charity parades

Hospitals up until the introduction of the National Health Service in 1948 had to raise funds by subscription and street collections. Many hospitals had charity days which took the form of a parade. All the local firms and societies would take a pride in producing the best-dressed float and a fancy dress parade was usually held. Prizes were awarded and the people would line the route cheering them on. Later there would be a picnic and in the evening a concert or a dance would be held.

Charity Schools Parade

Children in Glasgow who attended charity schools paraded annually on 26th of April - 600 in 1820, accompanied by the Magistrates, ministers and governors of the institutions in full dress. They marched from Hutchesons' Hospital to St Andrew's Church. After the service they returned to their own school to dine on roast beef, plum pudding and a drink to toast their founders.

Robin and Ian Strain, Kirkcaldy, on the shore of the Holy Loch, 1941.

Holidays

Those children who were taken on holiday might belong to the better off families who built large houses at the coast to which they transferred for a

Well-dressed for sailing model yachts at Seamill, 1920s.   J. Barr.

month or so at a time. They closed their town houses, sent the servants ahead and spent time in the country or at the seaside.

Other children might be lucky to be taken on holiday in a rented apartment or house. Families, including several generations as well as aunts, uncles and cousins would holiday together. If they did not want to cater for themselves they could take attendance which meant buying in the food but having a woman come in to cook it, serve it and clean up.

Travelling to the holiday resort meant getting dressed up in your best clothes. In the 1890s and up until World War One even on the beach formal clothing was worn. From the 1930s Clark's sandals and sandshoes were popular, bathing costumes, shorts and print dresses came in and the best clothes only appeared again for travelling home. Transport was by train, horse brake or steamer. Only the very well-off had their own motor car.

We arrived at Partick Pier far too early. The sun shone hotly; the tide was low; and it was before the days of Clyde purification. Not to be squeamish about it, the Clyde at Glasgow was then a big sewer. We and other families waited and waited. In the heat babies began to girn; small children grew peevish; little girls complained or looked pathetically patient. For the boys there was always the

entertainment of the shipping - liners, channel and river steamers, cargo vessels, barques, barquentines, brigs and schooners, dredgers, hoppers and ferries.

I Remember, J. J. Bell, 1932

Model yachts were sailed in paddling pools or in the sea, metal pails and spades were deadly weapons as well as for making sandpies and swimming in the sea required a chittery bite - a sandwich or biscuit - afterwards to ward off the cold. Bigger resorts would offer donkey rides along the sand.

Hydropathics

More like a punishment rather than a holiday was the stern regime of a hydropathic. This was a large castle-like hotel to which people went to benefit from the special properties of its water; another name for these was spas. The rooms were not centrally heated, there were no lifts and lights had to be out by 10.00pm. There was a warning bell sounded every morning at 8am so that no-one would miss breakfast.

There were prayers after breakfast in the lounge and a church service every evening. Laughter or singing were frowned on and any child who was tempted to slide along the highly polished floors was in trouble. Some wild boys would mix up the shoes left outside the room doors to be polished but if they were ever caught their parents would be

banned from booking again. Sometimes a game of spin-the-plate or skittles was allowed on a wet afternoon and croquet outside on a dry one.

Children were tolerated rather than welcomed. Under the age of eight all their meals were served in the nursery and under the age of twelve they were served tea at six o'clock in their bedroom and were not allowed in the public rooms in the evening so had to pass the time reading.

Social life

The main social life outside of the home was based on the church, youth organisations, sports and hobbies. There was little commercial entertainment.

Youth organisations

There were an enormous number of organisations to which young people could belong. Apart from the major youth movements and Sabbath schools, friendly societies, political parties, temperance associations all had clubs. The main aim was to provide a social and enjoyable environment for young people which kept them out of mischief and diverted their energies into useful and healthy pastimes. A number of these organisations gave their members the opportunity to camp, hike and try out water sports and other activities which they would not meet in their daily life.

Woodcraft Folk

Children were valued by the Co-operative Movement and encouraged to learn about its ideals. Local Societies ran Junior Guilds and Children's Circles. In the 1920s the Woodcraft Folk was formed. Its aims were similar to the Boy Scouts' but they were careful to avoid the marching and what they saw as the emphasis on soldiering of that organisation. Camping was used as a way of bringing young people into the Co-operative Movement although the Woodcraft Folk was an independent, auxiliary organisation. International exchanges were important as they allowed friendships to develop between young people of different cultures.

The Co-operative Youth Club

For teenagers who had outgrown the Woodcraft Folk the Co-operative Movement ran youth clubs which met for debates, discussion groups, drama, swimming and football as well as dancing.

The Boys' Brigade

The Boys' Brigade was founded in Glasgow by William Smith, a worker with the Woodside District Mission attached to the Free Church of Scotland. He was also an officer in the 1st Lanark Rifle Volunteers. To hold the interest of the older boys he thought up the idea of incorporating military style drill and discipline in a separate organisation. The 1st Glasgow Company of the The City Boys' Brigade drilled with real rifles.

Govan Boy Scouts' camp, 1920s.

classes, sports and hobbies, shooting practice, brass and pipe bands were also catered for and an interest in the outdoor life was introduced through camping.

By 1891 the Glasgow Battalion numbered 4,160 boys while throughout Scotland there were over ten thousand members. 3,649 of them were invited to form a guard of honour at the opening of the 1901 International Exhibition by the Prince and Princess of Wales.

suaded by Smith to write *Scouting for Boys*. The movement began in 1907 and was designed to appeal to boys who enjoyed the outdoor life. The 1st Glasgow claims to be the oldest Scottish group and there was a rapid expansion of troops throughout Scotland after the second national camp, which was held in 1908 at Hunshugh, Northumbria and attended by representatives of Scottish Scouts.

Packs of Cubs were also formed for the younger boys and Rovers for those over sixteen. Scout troops were sometimes attached to a church but they often had their own scout hall. They built trek carts in which they carried their tents. An early Bob-a-Job Week was held in 1914 called The Scouts Day of Work to raise funds for the National Institute for the Blind at Larbert. Scouts carried out all sorts of jobs including caddying on golf courses. The original uniform hat was a large bushranger type and they carried a wooden stave. Scottish Scouts were proud of the fact that they wore the kilt. They learned first aid as part of their programme.

B.B. camp kit inspection, 1940s.   Bill Findlay.

The Boys' Brigade began, in 1883, with thirty boys aged from twelve to seventeen. There were three officers. It was also intended that companies would be attached to a Christian organisation and many churches formed companies. Ambulance

Boy Scouts

Sir Robert Baden-Powell, hero of Mafeking, met with William Smith, founder of the Boys' Brigade, in a hotel in Glasgow and the idea for Scouting was born. He was per-

I was a member of the troop attached to St Mary's Episcopal Church in Great Western Road, Glasgow. We camped at Loch Tay, the first time being in 1913 when I was twelve. Although I was small I was a good swimmer and was one of a group of boys chosen to dive into the loch to ensure that it was safe for the non-swimmers to learn to swim.

Interview with Jack Peters, 1970

Singer Sewing Machines, Clydebank

Large firms often had a social side providing club and sports facilities for employees and their families. Singer, with its American patriarchal style, had so many employees that it could hold inter-departmental tournaments as well as compete elsewhere. The children of employees were also catered for and an annual Festival was held including an exhibition of crafts. Children were encouraged to take part and both boys and girls were commended for the high quality of work which they achieved. They and many firms, as well as towns and villages, held annual galas at which a young girl was chosen as Gala Queen and others as her attendants.

The Foundry Boys Society

This Society, despite its name was open to both boys and girls. Instituted in 1865 for the 'religious, educational and social elevation of the boys and girls of Glasgow' it had, in 1885, a membership of 19,000 looked after by 2,200 voluntary workers. It ran ninety branches and issued a magazine, *The Foundry Boy*, which it stressed was non-sectarian. It also ran a Penny Savings Bank and an annual Fair trip. In 1866, ninety boys and monitors sailed to Lochgoilhead and in 1886 they chartered a steamer to take 500 senior boys and girls to Mambeg.

Scottish Schoolboys' Club

Stanley Nairne inaugurated a Schoolboys' Missionary Camp, in 1912, with a weekend camp for twenty Edinburgh schoolboys held in a disused church at Mountaincross village. The idea spread to Glasgow and weekend camps were held annually despite the declaration of World War One.

School life was going on and, in spite of the war, boys had a life to look forward to, and it seemed all the more necessary

THE NEW WORLD — ITS FOUNDATIONS TO BE JUSTICE — LOVE TO BE THE SPIRIT OF ITS INHABITANTS

STUC Library.

because of the war to give boys the chance of experiencing all the things for which the camps stood...in April 1915, the barn at Cademuir resounded to the noise of over a hundred Edinburgh boys and about eighty Glasgow boys.

The Story of the Scottish Schoolboys' Club, 1912-1987, Stanley Nairne and David Williamson, 1987

From this grew the Scottish Schoolboys' Club. This Christian youth club provides the opportunity for boys, and since 1980 girls, to experience the joys of camping under canvas and the outdoor life while learning about the spiritual side of life. A permanent site was established in 1981 at Struan, Perthshire.

Political involvement

All the political parties including the Independent Labour Party had young people's groups. The Young Imperialists were a Conservative Party group who debated topics of the day such as '*Are women a success in business?*'

Miss Parker, president, spoke for the motion. Her points were that women had to break down the barriers of sex antagonism and lay low prejudices of men, they had proved their worth during the war when they undertook masculine duties and performed them successfully and these days could compete with men in every sphere of activity.

Mr. McCulloch spoke against the

motion. His points were that women were temperamentally unsuitable by reason of their greater emotional bias, were illogical and easily influenced and that the average length of time in business was ten years then she would marry. The motion was carried.

Clydebank Press, 4th May, 1924

The Boys of Empire, the Young Communists League, the Junior Guild of the Liberal Party and the Young Socialists were other attractions. This last ran a newsletter from 1901 entitled the *Young Socialist - a magazine of justice and love*. Its aims were to build a world-wide union of socialist children and included a moralistic fairy story. The magazine continued until 1979.

Sunday schools

The original Sunday schools of the eighteenth century were set up to teach reading and writing to poor children who had to work during the week. In 1800 the Sabbath Evening School Society was opened to bring young people to religion as an antidote to vice and to woo them from a life of crime. A juvenile library of suitable reading was available in most of their premises and Bibles and hymn books were in use. Scripture texts were distributed as rewards for good attendance, good conduct and hard work. In the early 1900s the Independent Labour Party ran non-religious Sunday schools.

Penny matinee, Edinburgh, 1925.

Christian Sunday schools under the supervision of the superintendent were attached to every church. The Beginners department was for pre-school children, the Juniors up until secondary age and the Seniors up to fourteen. The Salvation Army also ran Sunday schools as did The Railway Mission.

Temperance societies

From 1829 onwards junior branches of the various temperance societies were formed to beat the 'curse of the demon drink' as the drinking of alcohol was called. There children could learn about the evils caused by overindulgence in alcohol. The Band of Hope, the Little Ribboners, the Young Abstainers and the Catholic League of the Cross were some of these clubs. Magic lantern slides were shown usually telling the tragic story of waifs and strays left starving at the door of a public house while their parents spent their wages on drink. Soirees were held when songs were sung and a bag of buns was given to each child. Ungrateful boys were known to start a bun fight to the

annoyance of the superintendent. Children were urged to sign the pledge and swear: 'I agree, with the help of promised grace, to abstain from all intoxicating liquor, as a beverage.' Pledge cards were given out at a cost of one penny and entitled the owner to a night's entertainment and a sweetie and the chance to chant their own version of the pledge.

> Look on spirits as your foe
> Make your answer ever 'No'
> See the drunkards o'er the edge
> Keep yer heid and sign the pledge.

Traditional

Cinema

The cinemas brought 'canned' entertainment to everyone who lived near one. Firstly the films were silent, later sound was introduced then colour. Even fairly small towns would have more than one picture house. In Scotland going to see a film was usually known as 'going to the pictures'. The programmes changed up to three times a week and *Pathe News* specials kept people informed about important events. These, in

black and white, would be shown a few days after the actual date of a coronation or Royal wedding. The War was reported in this way.

Children had the ABC Club at cinemas on Saturday mornings but not just to entertain them. It also aimed to give them moral guidance through showing suitable films such as those made by the Children's Film Foundation. Every week the children gathered and sang this song before the performance began:

> We come along on Saturday morning
> Greeting everybody with a smile.
> We come along on Saturday morning
> Knowing that it's well worth while.
> As members of the ABC,
> We all intend to be
> Good citizens when we grow up
> And champions of the free.
> We come along on Saturday morning
> Greeting everybody with a smile,
> Smile, smile.
> Greeting everybody with a smile.

As remembered by Bob Dawson, 1997

Some cinemas admitted children on production of an empty jam jar which in those days was returnable like lemonade bottles and money could be had for handing them in to shops.

Hobbies

Hobbies such as collecting postage stamps, birds eggs and butterflies were taken up by boys. Both boys and girls took part in Highland dancing competitions held at Highland Games. Up until the 1960s girls wore the full kilted outfit rather than the white blouse, tartan skirt and laced waistcoat. Classes in ballet, tap dancing and ballroom dancing were popular from 1900. Etiquette was also learned and boys had to bow to their partners and girls had to curtsey at the end of each dance.

76th Glasgow B.B. swimming trophy, 1915.

Sports

Better off children and country children had ponies to ride on. Skating took place on lochs when the ice was thick enough. Public swimming baths were opened in the 1880s and 1890s enabling more children to learn to swim. At school boys played soccer and rugby and girls hockey, netball and lacrosse. Tennis became popular as local authorities provided courts in the public parks and a few children had access to golf and cricket clubs.

The Midshipmite operetta, 1940s.   Bill Findlay.

Music

Instrumental

Children were members of brass, flute and pipe bands. Many children spent hours practising at the piano and sitting 'grades' as the exams of the London School of Music were called or scraping away on the violin. It was considered a social grace, in middle-class circles, to be able to 'do a turn' to entertain your parents' friends at a social evening at home.

Choirs

Many children were members of junior choirs which as well as giving concerts often took part in competitions where the adjudicators awarded marks and doled out criticism of their efforts. Other children took part in the Gaelic Mod hoping to win medals.

We were in a junior choir which was run by Mrs Falconer and her sister Miss Stevenson in Eastbank Church. You didn't need to be a member of that church to join. Every year there was a concert in the church hall. The first part was ordinary singing, standing in rows but the bit we liked best was the second half because we got dressed up and had our faces covered with cocoa like minstrels. We danced and acted out popular songs.

It always ended up with a big

scene representing the songs of England, Scotland, Ireland and Wales. We dressed in national costumes and waved flags. Britannia came on last. She wore a lovely white dress and stood up high. We sang 'All men must be free', 'Rule Britannia' and finished with 'Land of Hope and Glory'. The people clapped like mad.

Interview with Margaret Gibson , 1982

Girls' pipe band, Muir of Ord, 1940s.

Kinderspiels

These were full blown musicals with costumes, scenery, make-up and stage lighting. They had titles like *The King of Kandy, Princess of Poppyland, The Magic Ruby* and *The Feast of Saint Hans.* There were three acts and four part singing choruses as well as solo parts, and dancing. Material was scarce during World War Two and old blueprints were boiled to rescue the linen which was made into costumes for the dancers.

Health

The health of children was not of any great consideration in the middle decades of the nineteenth century. Illness was treated the same whether adults or children were the sufferers. Many cures which were relied on were herbal or even pure superstition.

Coughs were remedied by infusing a syrup of holly bark or a potion of harts-tongue boiled with St John's Wort and ale. The juice from ivy leaves was inhaled to relieve catarrh and thyme cured whooping cough. Many other cures relied on natural substances. Camphor was placed in a bag and hung around the neck to cure sciatica. Salt was heated and placed in a woollen sock which was put against the face to cure gumboils or toothache. A sweaty sock was wrapped around the neck to cure a sore throat. Whisky was dropped onto a sore tooth or put on a piece of cotton wool and placed in the mouth and treacle and sulphur were used to cure several ailments. A paste of fern leaves mixed with white of egg and an infusion made from ivy leaves healed sore eyes.

All calls by or visits to a doctor had to be paid for and so he, for it was usually a man, was only sent for as a last resort. Although many working-class families paid into health schemes via a friendly society, sending for a doctor or attempting to consult one was not an easy task before 1948. Complaints arose because of the red tape which was necessary before a patient could be seen. A line had to be obtained from the secretary of the friendly society or, in the case of the free parish doctor, from the inspector of the poor. The Parish Council office was only open from 9.30am to 5.30pm and a doctor would not call without this piece of paper being presented at his surgery. Before the National Insurance Act of 1911 there was no provision made nationally for those who were ill or in need of medical attention. After this Act the person in work was covered for treatment but not his family, except for tuberculosis or maternity cases.

As early as the Factory Act of 1802 mention was made of the dread, especially in the rapidly expanding towns, of infectious disease. The cramped living conditions, lack of sanitation and poor nutrition allowed these diseases to spread but no action was taken. At Elgin Colliery, Dunfermline, an outbreak of scarlatina, in 1861, killed many children. Children died of pneumonia, diptheria, meningitis, asthma and other respiratory diseases. As the century progressed so did tuberculosis, causing a headache for the authorities.

Sanitary conditions or lack of them in most towns were beginning to be recognised as contributing to disease. Recommendations were made in the 1860s after reports on children in reformatories and poorhouses showed them to be puny and argued that they should have more exposure to fresh air and more use should be made of play areas.

Certain illnesses and deformities were associated with working in conditions which were injurious to health. The long hours, hard work and poor nourishment led to bone deformities such as knock-knees, bow-legs and damaged spines and to respiratory diseases from the lack of fresh air and the abundance of dust.

The Children's Employment Commission of 1863 found children of six working in a match factory filling wooden frames with phosphorous matches. This caused a disease which rotted their teeth and jaws. Work in a factory, such as a tannery, which used chrome dust could lead to a wearing away of the bridge of the nose and the skin around it. Climbing boys developed lung cancer from constantly breathing in soot and skin cancer was also a hazard.

In 1875, a Factory Act Commission taking evidence found that small children were employed in shipbuilding. They were put into the tubes to hold the ends of the rivets, and in consequence of the great noise echoing around them, the drums of the children's ears split and they became permanently deaf.

Under the Education (Scotland) Act 1908, day schools and classes for 'defective children, epileptics, cripples, myopic, blind and deaf aged from five to sixteen' were opened in major towns and the Medical Officer of Health could recommend pupils to attend. A scale of fees existed based on the parents' ability to pay and needy children were enrolled free. Sight-saving classes were provided and stammerers were catered for after normal school hours.

Deaf and dumb

As early as 1760 there was an institution in Edinburgh for the treatment and care of those unfortunate enough to be deaf and unable to speak. This was the first of its kind in Britain. The Duke of Buccleuch and Queensferry in 1810 established, in Edinburgh, an Institution for the Instruction of Deaf and Dumb Children. In 1816 there were forty nine pupils learning reading, arithmetic, writing and recitation. Subscribers would visit the school and remark on the quality of the pupils' work.

One boy wrote, 'the Lady and

Gentleman is love (sic) look at Deaf and Dumb Institution last Wednesday.' The pupils were also paraded around Scotland to show the progress which had been made and to raise further funds. It was common practice to exhibit children from institutions in this way.

As the century progressed Deaf and Dumb Missions and institutions were established in most major cities. In 1860 the Board of Supervision for the Poor Law was required by law to provide instruction for deaf and dumb pauper children. Dundee paid capitation fees and gave grants to the Dundee Mission to the Deaf and Dumb.

Mental illness

There was no attempt made in Victorian times to shield people suffering from mental illness from embarrassment. The language used was plain and descriptive - idiot, cretin, imbecile, feeble-minded and defective were the terms used to describe those unfortunates in need of care.

In 1853, Sir John and Lady Ogilvie privately paid for an institution at Baldovan, Dundee. The Scottish National Institution for the Training of Imbeciles was opened in Edinburgh in 1866. Private cases paid fees while public assistance cases received free training.

A few gentlemen, stimulated by the efforts of Dr Guggenbuhl amongst the cretins of Switzerland, commenced a small institution in Edinburgh for the education of imbeciles, which was afterwards [1880] *transferred to the district of Larbert.* [Set up for the] *Children of poor parents who are unable to do anything either for them or with them...There were 71 male and 41 female inmates over 6 years of age.* [Accommodation existed for 200 - 250.] *A considerable space is allotted to playgrounds, bright with gowans and buttercups and bearing plenty of grass for the little feeble folk to tumble in.*

A History of Stirlingshire, James Nimmo, 1900

In 1870, the new City Poorhouse at Craiglockhart, Edinburgh, opened and accepted 'lunatic pauper' children. In 1897 the Barony Parish Council, Glasgow, sanctioned the building of a special home for children incapable of being educated.

In 1900 Glasgow District Lunacy Board opened a Home for Imbecile Children at Woodilee Asylum, Lenzie. Detached from the main Asylum buildings it was a substantial building in the Italian style, consisting of three storeys with playrooms, dormitories, lavatories, and having its own hospital for six patients. A description of the opening was given in newspapers of the time of how the company who attended the opening were conveyed by special train from Glasgow to Lenzie and thence by brake to Woodilee and of the decor of the building but the only words about the children to be written were that it catered for thirty-five 'helpless and hopeless' souls.

In the 1900s The Glasgow Association of Defective and Feeble-minded Children opened a training school at Kirkintilloch to educate and train girls from five to sixteen years of age. St Charles' Certified Institution was opened at Carstairs for the same age group under the supervision of the Sister Superior.

Old Kilpatrick Care Committee

This body was a voluntary one which helped young people over sixteen with mental illness to find employment and also provided education for so-called 'ineducable' children. The children attended Milton Special School. Children were discharged from special schools at the age of sixteen.

Physical handicap

The Education (Scotland) Act 1872 introduced school attendance officers who enquired into the non-attendance of children of school age. This revealed that many children were unable physically to attend their local school. It was decided to provide a special home where the children could also be educated.

East Park Home

The School Board of Glasgow co-operated with a group of volunteer lady visitors who collected subscriptions and raised funds to enable them to establish a special place where physically handicapped children could be both taught and cared for in pleasant surroundings. East Park Home for Infirm Children, purpose built in 1874 at Maryhill, Glasgow, was the result. It combined hospital facilities with everyday activities. Children lived in wards and the staff wore nurses' uniform. Many improvements were made in artificial aids. New limbs, crutches and wheelchairs were introduced.

East Park Home, 1930s.
Heatherbank Museum of Social Work.

An appeal was made regularly to children to give money for the upkeep of Eastpark Home and also to their parents.

Oh! you, whose little children,
Are lapped in loving care,
Whose homes are nests of luxury,
Whose lives are bright and fair,
Think of those darker dwellings
Where comforts never come,
Out of your own rich treasuries
Give to the Children's Home!

Eastpark Home Appeal booklet

The Invalid and Crippled Children's Aid Association

Postcards picturing handicapped children were sold for people to send to friends. They were looked on as freaks and were gawped at in the street. The Elim Church opened a home for boys in 1891 and The Invalid and Crippled Children's Aid Association, which began in 1893, sent children with physical handicaps on holiday to Abernyte. In 1919 it bought a home at Rattray and there was a Children's Home and Hospital at Strathblane. The Association also offered help and advice to parents on coping with a handicappped child.

Mary Lily Walker of the Dundee Social Union set up a school for invalids at Grey Lodge in the city which later moved to more suitable premises. In 1906 it came under the School Board becoming the foundation of one of the first special schools which was opened in 1914.

Princess Margaret Rose Orthopaedic Hospital

In November 1925, an Edinburgh Rotarian, Dr T. Radcliffe Barnett, gave a talk called *The problem of the crippled child.* It was estimated that in Fife and the Lothians there were 1,000 crippled children under twelve years of age and 353 identified in the thirteen to sixteen age group within Edinburgh alone. Rickets, tuberculosis, polio and other bone deformities were common and the availability of physiotherapy treatment was inadequate.

The Rotary Club of Edinburgh agreed to organise a fund-raising campaign called 'To every child a chance,' to establish three twenty-five bed wards to be named The Edinburgh Hospital for Crippled Children. H.R.H. The Duchess of York, now The Queen Mother, laid the foundation stone in August 1929 and the hospital, when officially opened in June 1933, received the name Princess Margaret Rose Orthopaedic Hospital after her younger daughter who was born at Glamis Castle, Angus. Two of the wards were to be open-air wards for the treatment of children with tuberculosis of the hip and other joints.

The first patient was thirteen years old receiving treatment for osteomylitis at the time and had been under the care of Mr William

Cochrane in ward 13 of Edinburgh Royal Infirmary for about two years. He was in the new hospital for eighteen months. Only wards 1 and 2 were in use at first and they had only three sides, being completely open to the south at all times. In winter the top covering of the beds was a brown canvas sheet which was necessary as there was often snow on the beds after a storm.

Hospitals

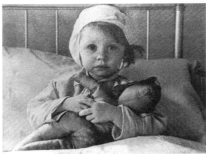

Child with rag doll, 1920s.   Ken Willox.

Edinburgh Sick Children's Hospital

Until well into the nineteenth century treatment for many children could only be sought in a voluntary hospital, which was free, or in the poorhouse infirmary. In Edinburgh, in 1860 a decision was taken to open subscriptions for a hospital which would specialise in caring for sick children. A house was leased in Lauriston Lane, against the wishes of the neighbours. It was converted into wards and twelve patients were admitted. There was also an out patients clinic. A Ladies Committee drummed up practical support, collecting clothing and equipment.

In 1863 the hospital moved to Meadowside House where it could cater for a wider range of diseases. Nevertheless there were no facilities for surgical cases. A further move was necessary, in 1879, to expand the facilities and to include an operating theatre. Morningside Academy, a private school for boys and previously a hydropathic, became Plewlands House then in 1895, after another move, it become the Royal Hospital for Sick Children.

Glasgow Hospital for Sick Children

In 1861 one hundred and seventy one children were treated at Glasgow Royal Infirmary. Dr Gairdner, Glasgow's first Medical Officer of Health, in 1863 advocated the idea that sick children should be treated separately but found no support either amongst fellow medics or the public. Although Beatrice Clugston had held a bazaar in 1867 to raise money to provide for a Convalescent Fever Home for Sick Children it was not until 1882 that a hospital catering for the needs of sick children was opened in Glasgow. An old house was converted as a hospital with wards and theatres.

The windows were colourfully painted with nursery rhyme figures the cost of which came from money subscribed by children. The walls were half-tiled in cream with a red border. There was a kitchen and bathroom, an isolation ward - with its own nurse - and fifty eight cots, as the beds in the wards were called, were installed. A mortuary decorated in marble where parents could hold the funeral service if they wished completed the building.

Admission was by individuals and institutions subscribers' lines but G.P.s and visitors of the poor could also send weak or rickety children for treatment. On arrival all children were bathed. Some cried, 'I'll be drooned' as they had never been in a bath before. Day and night dresses were made by the sewing group of Hyndland Parish Church. The first patient was a five year old boy who was operated on and successfully treated for curvature of the spine. Many patients were treated for bow-legs, caused by rickets, and knock-knees; these conditions were the result of malnutrition.

Drumchapel

A country branch with twenty four cots in two wards which also had sun rooms and a theatre was opened at Drumchapel in 1903. This catered especially for children with tuberculosis of the hip joint. Children were driven there from the city by a horse-drawn bus.

Hospital Charities Day, 1930s, Kirkintilloch. East Dunbartonshire Libraries.

Fund raising

Fund raising took place throughout the west of Scotland and as far north east as Banff and children from all over Scotland were treated. In 1885 the Scottish Football Association first donated the takings from the Glasgow Charity Cup, the *People's Friend* annually held a knitting and crocheting competition and the entries were donated to the hospital and Cumbrae Band of Hope denied themselves sweets during the summer of 1887 and donated 18/7d. A bazaar was held to raise funds for new, purpose built premises at Yorkhill House and £15,000 was raised. It opened in July 1914. For £2,000 a ward could have the donor's name engraved above the doorway, for £100 a cot could have a plaque with the donor's name above the bed. Hutchesons' Girls Grammar School had a permanent Cot-Box collection box to help the school to maintain its cot in the hospital.

Dispensary

From 1888 the hospital had run a free dispensary, a clinic which also made up and distributed medicines, where children could be brought for examination. Help was also given to pay for a funeral, advice was freely given on child care and many parents brought their children to the dispensary who would never have gone to a doctor's surgery. Treats were given to children at Christmas and in 1918 140 attended the pantomime.

Dundee Infants Hospital

As a result of pressure by the Dundee Social Union an infants' hospital was planned in 1915 but it was five years later before the roomy house, The Lodge, Broughty Ferry was renovated and officially opened in February 1920 by the Countess of Airlie. Dr Burgess, Dundee's Medical Officer of Health said that this hospital was needed in Dundee because few towns had a higher infant mortality rate. Two hundred and twenty children were treated in the first year. In the first annual report it was regretted that some infants had relapses because of the poor conditions to which they had to return on discharge. By 1925 the hospital was in financial difficulties. The report of that year stated that only sixty six subscribers remained and that contributions from empoyees in industry had fallen away.

Education

Many children spent a long time in hospital and missed out on their schooling. Although there was a proposal in 1912 to appoint teachers to children's hospitals, in the majority of general hospitals this did not become established until 1923. Class teaching with up to thirty pupils per class and two sessions per day was provided.

Treatment of infectious diseases

Infectious disease was the greatest fear of all. It was not always understood that these diseases, mainly fevers, could be passed on through direct contact and so they spread quickly, more and more cases developing in a small area. Some children believed that to avoid catching an infectious disease all that was necessary was to recite these words if you saw an ambulance or fever van, as it was called:

> *touch your collar, never swallow, never get the fever. touch your nose, touch your toes, never go in one of those*

then you had to spit on the ground.

Vermin

The wearing of second hand clothing was a factor in the transference of body lice. The body louse was common and verminous children were discovered in great numbers after the Education (Scotland) Act 1908 introduced compulsory medical inspection of all school children and the School Health Service began. It was not, however, until 1913 that it was recognised as a carrier of infectious disease.

Head lice were also virulent and were passed on in the classroom. They liked clean hair in which to lay their eggs and no child was immune.

> *I had long thick plaits which were cut off the day that nits were found in my hair and I never had long hair again. My mother bought Derbac soap and Dettol. A fine bone comb was used to force the eggs to lose their grip and there was a cracking sound as they were put onto the china saucer of disinfectant. Nearly everyone in the class had to be treated.*

Interview with Sheila Peters, 1997

Notification

In 1874 School Boards interchanged information of cases of infectious disease on an informal basis. The Infectious Disease (Notification) Act 1889 gave warning of an epidemic and allowed the Medical Officer of Health to take appropriate steps such as closing schools. The Public Health Act 1897 made notification compulsory.

Measles occurred mainly in infant departments of schools but no provision was made to include this disease for notification until 1901. Death rates for young children were high in 1886, 1908 and 1922. Older children in a family where measles was diagnosed were excluded from attending school.

Nurseries

Some people felt that nurseries were breeding grounds for infectious disease. This was not borne out by statistics which showed that children attending them were usually taller, heavier and brighter than average. Nursery staff took the children to the nearest park for fresh air where possible.

Nursery nurses with their charges.

Vaccination

When first introduced, an organised programme of vaccination against smallpox carried out by the Faculty of Physicians and Surgeons was frowned upon and seen as an interference with the will of God. Nevertheless in 1801, the Glasgow Faculty of Physicians and Surgeons appointed two doctors to attend at the Faculty Hall every Monday to vaccinate the children of the poor without charge.

Year	No of children vaccinated against smallpox
1801-1811	14,500
1812	950
1813	1,162
1814	875
1815	926
1816 [Jan. to May]	568
Total	**18,981**

For each child to be vaccinated the parent deposited 2/- against a return visit when the child's arm was inspected by the attending surgeon to take away any matter which may have gathered. The money was then refunded.

In 1835-39 when vaccination was optional, children under ten years of age made up 93% of deaths due to smallpox. In the epidemic of 1855, 89% of deaths came into this category. Under the Vaccination

(Scotland) Act 1864 vaccination was made compulsory and the effectiveness of the programme was shown by a fall in the death rate of children under ten to 38% in the epidemic of 1870-72 and to 16% in 1900-1902.

Under the Vaccination (Scotland) Act 1907 a clause was introduced which recognised the right of parents to register as conscientious objectors. Parish and Town Councils kept a register of children granted exemption which revealed that the ratio was one in four of all children eligible. This was reflected in the rise to 29% of deaths of children under ten in the epidemic of 1920.

Polio

There were two forms of polio - poliomylitis, better known as infantile paralysis because it attacked the spinal chord, and polio encephalitis which attacked the lining of the brain. The first cases occurred in well cared for children in Clackmannanshire in 1911. In Aberdeen in 1916 there was an outbreak of seventy nine cases between April and September resulting in the death of four children. A further outbreak occurred in 1919 and was linked to the influenza epidemic. Throughout Scotland children were suffering from these diseases of the nervous system and an epidemic occurred in the autumn of 1928. It began to be recognised that it was most likely

that the number of cases might increase during the second half of the year. A theory that flies were carriers was investigated.

During the summer of 1944 there were major outbreaks and all swimming pools were closed down as a precautionary measure. It was thought that the water could spread the disease. Children were treated in an iron lung, a casing which covered the whole body and took over their breathing.

Diptheria

This disease also seemed to become widespread after the school holidays. It was thought at one time that the use of communal lead cups at drinking wells and the sharing at school of wooden lead pencils could spread the infection. Immunisation against diptheria was introduced in 1940 and this led to a rapid disappearance of the disease.

I was taken to Belvidere Hospital in the fever van. It was in 1911 when I was eight and I was terrified because my long hair, which I was proud of being able to sit on when it wasn't in pleats, was shaved off. I didn't know that it would grow in again. Nobody explained why this had to happen and I cried for hours. I wanted to see my mother but no-one was allowed to visit you. My sisters were angry because I had been playing with a wooden dolly which our great uncle, Tom Goslan, had made for us and the sanitary men burned it along with many of our books, rag dolls and other toys. They used sulphur to fumigate the rooms of your house.

Interview with Margaret Peters, 1986

Many patients required surgery which involved opening an airway in the throat. This was called a tracheotomy. In spite of this action many children died.

Scarlet fever

A stay in hospital of six weeks was usual for scarlet fever and patients were isolated. Families could only bring parcels to be handed in at the gatehouse and sometimes children could wave to their parents through the railings.

I had never been away from home when without understanding why I was taken to Lightburn Hospital. There were other children in the ambulance and we were all crying which annoyed the nurse. The food was awful. I hate gravy and wouldn't eat until my mother explained to them that if they gave me my potatoes dry I would be happier. I never saw my parents for six weeks. They would come up and hand in comics and a few sweeties. All the sweets were pooled in the ward and shared out because it was war-time and they were rationed. I was six, so it must have been in 1943. If they brought any books or toys these had to be left there. You couldn't take them home.

The awful thing was that you didn't feel ill yet you stayed in bed for days before you were allowed to play in the dayroom. Once we were sent outside to play and a wee girl saw her brother who was in the dysentry ward and rushed over to hug him. She was kept isolated from everyone in case she would pass it on. It was a terrible experience, not like the bright, cheery wards they have today.

Interview with Sheila Peters, 1997

There were skipping rhymes about being in hospital as it was a shared experience identified by many children.

It's weeks and weeks, and days and days,
Since I've seen my home.
Father, mother, take me away from this convalescent home.

Traditional

Tuberculosis

Sanatoria were built in the country for the treatment of children suffering from tuberculosis. In 1912 an experiment took place in Glasgow and Edinburgh where Preventoria were built in the country for the

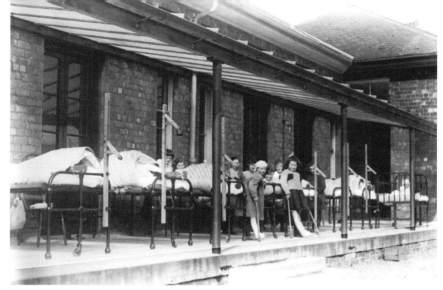

Children suffering from TB, Robroyston Hospital, 1930s.   Heatherbank Museum of Social Work.

residential treatment of children. The School Board would supply teaching staff so that the patients could continue their schooling. Biggart Memorial Home, Prestwick even had an open-air school.

Mountblow bairns.
West Dunbartonshire Libraries.

Convalescent homes

Many charities set up homes for children recovering from illness or operations. These were usually run by a matron and a qualified nursing staff but were financed through fund raising committees whose members were often ladies of means with time to spare to devote to this cause.

St Leonard's School Seniors Children's Convalescent Home

The 'Seniors', the name used to describe former pupils of St Leonard's School for Girls, St Andrews, collected money to open a home for convalescent children. They rented accommodation from Woodburn Laundry and this house was in use from 1903-1908 when

they raised sufficient funds to build a new purpose built Home close to the school. It catered for twelve children aged from four - twelve years with an average stay of a month. Many suffered from rickets.

Their cheerful voices fill the air with a rich mixed flavour of Edinburgh, Glasgow and Dundee, and all are busy with their own jobs. One small person...pushes a doll in a pram, an elder girl minds her little brother, for boys are admitted from four to six years old; others are playing at shop (which they love); all are busy and happy.

The Gazette, St Leonard's School Magazine, 1920

Each child was recommended by a Senior who paid its railway fare. The parents, if possible, were asked to pay a token 2/6d per week which only covered the cost of the child's milk. The Home catered for many children over the years but closed in 1955 when there was less need of its services after the introduction of the National Health Service.

The Georges' Wedding Gift Fund

In 1934 The Georges' Wedding Gift Fund was set up on the occasion of the wedding of Prince George, Duke of Kent, to H.R.H. Princess Marina. An appeal was made to all those in the west of Scotland whose name was George to subscribe to this fund which was to provide, through a Trust Fund, holidays for convalescent sick children of the unemployed.

Welfare

Until the nineteenth century, Scotland's poor were the responsibility of the church and of voluntary institutions and societies. After the Poor Law (Scotland) Act 1845, which was still effective in 1944, the onus fell upon the Parochial Boards of Parish Councils to provide for orphan, separated or deserted children. Often the solution was to house them in the local workhouse, or as it was known in Scotland, 'the poorhouse'.

Before this Act however, there were only thirteen poorhouses in Scotland, and the accommodation of such children along with adults was considered by many people as unsatisfactory.

A Government Commission of Enquiry reported in 1843 that in one poorhouse thirty five children under five were in a nursery with no toys and that in others the teachers employed were not qualified and were only acting as child minders.

Many more poorhouses were built by the state to house those coming under the new law. By 1865 there were sixty four operating which remained in existence until the repeal of the Act in 1928. Nevertheless, there were still, in 1900, 14% of children registered under the Poor Law living in poorhouses. The poorhouse was often seen as convenient for orphan children and a 'nursery for good servants'. Orphans could be purchased, technically called 'handing over for care', for a one-off payment of £25.

In 1881, at Linlithgow the Board of Supervision of the Poor in Scotland reported on the physical condition of children living in the poorhouse and recommended that more 'active and joyous games' should be introduced and that the children should be taken out for exercise two or three times per week.

Scottish Poor Law Association

Dr Norman Macleod, as parish minister of the area in which Barnhill Poorhouse, Glasgow was built in 1854 to house up to 2,000 'inmates', was shocked to find that there were many pauper children kept there. Despite the fact that there was a schoolroom and a separate children's section he did not consider it to be a suitable environment for them. He decided that a system of boarding out of these children in the homes of decent country folk would be the answer and also proposed the system of industrial farms which did eventually come into being at a much later date.

Boarding out

It is a well-known fact that the majority of such as are fond of boarding pauper children are attached more by desire to make a profit than to study the welfare of their charge.

Poor Law Magazine and Parochial Journal, 1864-1865

The writer of this article felt that keeping children in the poorhouse compelled them to be obedient and ensured that they were free of vermin.

A report published in 1869 showed that children who were boarded out rarely became a burden on the Poor Law later in life. In 1869, Sir John McNeill, Board of Supervision for Scotland, giving evidence to the Select Committee of the House of Commons stated that to send pauper children to the industrial schools was to stamp them as wrong-doers and he recommended boarding out. He also did not approve of schools which were attached to the poorhouse:

I want pauper children to mix with a better class of children if I can manage it. I do not want to intensify these pauper ideas by congregating them together.

Children of the State, F. Davenport and F. Fowke, 1889

Mr Hay, Governor of Dundee Poorhouse, also preferred sending children to the country as they became healthier and appeared cleverer. Strangers were usually better foster parents than relatives who often exploited the children, using them as cheap labour.

There was often a problem with Irish children who were Roman Catholics as there were fewer Catholic families in country places although they were sometimes sent to the Western Isles. The Smyllum Orphanage was opened in Lanark by the Roman Catholic Diocese in 1896. This institution catered especially for physically handicapped children and blind children.

Problems

Boarded out children on Iona were accused by the factor of the Duke of Argyll, in 1869, of pestering strangers 'by running after them and insisting on their buying pebbles, shells, seaweed etc.' and he demanded that they be located elsewhere. The accusation is refuted by Glasgow City Parish who were irked by the action of the Duke.

We would not have complained had they [the children] been objected to at first but knowingly to have permitted them to remain for eight years, during which time ties of the most tender kind were formed between the child and the foster parent, as all of them were to be adopted after they were twelve or thirteen years of age... And then without note or warning Mr. C [Campbell - the Duke's factor] with one dash of the pen, orders their instant dismissal, the scenes that took place on the day of separation may be imagined.

City Parish Minutes, Glasgow, 1st September, 1869

The boarding out system was eventually copied by England as being the most successful way of coping with disadvantaged children. By 1880 there were 5,133 children boarded out in Scotland but in 1890 this number had fallen to 4,998.

Children have adapted themselves to the conditions of the homes in which they have been boarded, easily and naturally, and on arrival at the age of puberty have gone out to such employments as were available in the districts in which they were placed. They have behaved themselves well and looked upon their guardians practically as their parents, and where not engaged as domestic servants, have made their guardians' houses their homes.

Poor Law Magazine and Parochial Journal, vol. 7, 1879

The children who were the responsibility of Edinburgh Parish Council, in 1900, were supplied every year with clothing. For boys: 1 cap, 1 pair braces, 2 handkerchiefs, 2 scarves, 2 semmits, 2 pair of woollen hose, 2 shirts, 1 suit, 1 pair of cord trousers.

For girls: 2 chemises, 2 pair of drawers, 1 hat, 2 handkerchiefs, 1 plaiding petticoat, 2 scarves, 2 semmits, 1 set of stays, 2 pair of woollen hose, 2 yards of body lining, cloth for 1 dress, print for 2 pinafores, buttons and 1½ yards of ribbon.

Not every family landed lucky and many were permanently damaged by their experiences. In 1864 six pauper children were found to be boarded out in a single apartment house.

The Depression

During the Depression in the 1930s poverty drove many families to allow their children to be boarded out as they believed that this was an opportunity to give them a better life. Margaret Borland was one of a family of ten - six girls and four boys. Her parents couldn't cope with them all and agreed to send seven of them to the Highlands to be happy.

We walked across the river to the Tent Hall in Glasgow and were given a plate of soup. There were hundreds of children gathered there. We were taken to Ward 24, Stobhill Hospital where a Miss Kippen was in charge. Next we went by train from Queen Street Station to Inverness and on to the Black Isle by taxi. We were split up. At first five of us were together but the folk found it too much and my sister Alice and I went to another croft. Our childhood years were spent grovelling in the soil. Before school, at Ferintosh, we had to rise at 6am and work in the byre. We walked to school while the bus passed us. We were never even given a 1d to let us take it in bad weather.

The people who boarded us were given 12/6 per week for each of us and two sets of clothing per year. Though they spoke to us in English when anyone came to the house they spoke in Gaelic so that we would not understand. I never saw my mother or father again. My mother died when twins were born not long after we left. She didn't have enough to eat. Many of the boarded out children were starved. Jean and Jim Nelson were so hungry that they cycled four miles and broke into a wee shop to find something to eat.

When Alice and I were fourteen we were sent to a Training School in Newton Stewart to learn to be domestics. We were clever enough but we never had a chance. I worked for three years for the Provost for £1 per

month and I remember buying a green skirt at Rowan and Borlands and a wee jar of Snofire vanishing cream with my first wage. Alice worked at the Temperance Hotel and was so unhappy that she and another girl ran away and walked all the way to Glasgow. Another cousin, Annie Petrie, was sent to a home at Maryhill and she just disappeared. We have often tried to find out about her but there is no information. She might have been sent abroad.

Interview with Margaret Borland [Magee], Kirkcudbright, 1997

The Parochial Boards tried not to separate families if possible but this sometimes resulted in them having to leave the area of their birth. Stobhill Hospital, Glasgow had a unit for children who were waiting to be fostered. The average stay there was three months. Four children from the Brown family of Dennistoun were put up for fostering after their mother died and their father could not cope. They were housed in Stobhill then taken round thirty two houses but no-one in Glasgow was willing to accept them all. They ended up with a woman in Peterhead who had recently lost her son. She had a daughter and another boy whom she was fostering whom she later adopted. She agreed to keep the Brown family together and although she was strict she was kind.

On their way home from school they collected wood shavings to help with the smoking of the herring. They were given Parish clothing - navy blue and red jumpers, navy and red socks, navy blue skirt or trousers and a pair of brogues. They were inspected every six months but they were not allowed direct contact with their father and could only write to him through the Councillors at John Street, Glasgow. Eventually after their father remarried they reluctantly returned to Glasgow.

Village Home System

Other arrangements for the care and accommodation of children included the building of large area or district schools in order to keep the children separate from adults or placing children in cottages in parties of between ten and thirty under the supervision of industrial teachers and superintendents. This latter scheme was called the Village Home System and was first adopted by Dr Barnardo at Ilford. In 1895, Mrs Greenlees, an appointee of Govan Parish Council, set up a deputation to visit cottage homes in Leeds, Bradford and Sheffield and was 'much pleased' with what she saw. Lady Inspectors and local ladies' visiting committees were set up to investigate this scheme further. In Scotland in 1898 there were 2,861 orphans, 1,231 deserted children and 1,708 separated from their parents.

Adoption

The Scottish Poor Law Association tried to have children adopted but came to the conclusion that 'people of the superior working-class will not take pauper children for payment' and declared that Parish Councils were reluctant to make a feature of disposing of such children in this way. The Association issued an appeal for adoptive parents as this would take children off the public rates. A guarantee was given that orphan children would be available but 'any child who turned out from moral, mental or physical defects to be undesirable' to the adoptive parents could be given back to the Parish Council for institutional treatment. The church was behind this move. Some children who were initially fostered were later adopted by their foster parents.

Orphanages

Several philanthropists, men and women who had wealth, and who wanted to use it to benefit the community, often gifted, built or renovated homes for orphans and maintained them. Societies and organisations, usually supported by voluntary subscriptions and collections, also ran orphanages while Parochial Boards, up until 1900, sometimes placed orphans in the poorhouse or in a separate unit paid for by the parish.

Dean Orphan Hospital

In 1727 through private donations an Orphan Hospital was proposed for Edinburgh. It was established in 1733 in a rented house and catered for thirty children. In 1735 they were transferred to a purpose built building in the Nor'loch Valley. In 1833 this became a home for poor and neglected charity children on a further move by the Orphan Hospital and Workhouse to a site near Dean Bridge. There two hundred children could be accommodated, maintained and given free education. It also took in boarders who paid £6 per year if a boy and £14 per year if a girl. In 1825, Cauvins Orphanage was

"Before & after", Quarrier's Homes, 1877. Heatherbank Museum of Social Work.

opened in Edinburgh by a teacher of French under an endowment 'for the support and education of orphan boys'.

Aberlour

At Aberlour in 1876 an orphanage opened, under the auspices of the Scottish Episcopal Church, with four boys but by 1902 there were 300 boys and girls living there in a small village under the wardenship of Canon Jupp.

Dean Wolfe was its warden from 1928-1958 including the years of the Depression in the 1930s when many children of parents who simply could not cope accepted the charity of this institution. Twins, Leonard and Dorothy, aged ten, were reluctantly placed in his care by their widowed father.

We [the girls] *sang as we sat busily mending the clothes of the inmates. We loved sad songs not because we were miserable but possibly because of their emotional appeal. We were well treated and had warm beds and good wholesome food. The dormitories were lit by gaslight.*

Adapted from *Haste Ye Back*, Dorothy Haynes, 1973

The Elgin Institution

The Elgin Institution was endowed in 1832 by Major-General Andrew Anderson of the Honorary East India Company. A sculpture of him giving bread to an elderly woman with one hand and holding out a book to a boy and girl with the other was placed outside. Fifty children were housed there up until they were apprenticed or sent out to service and there was also a free school for them and for other children of the town whose parents were poor but could still afford to keep them at home and clothe them.

Magdalen Asylums were accused of being of more benefit to speculators than to the orphan girls in their care. One observer wrote in the *Poor Law Magazine*, 1864-65 that he preferred a well conducted school in a poorhouse for such girls where they:

should be taught their letters without delay... then hired out to some employment, which in time will help them to earn their bread and butter and become self-supporting.

Quarriers Homes, boys learning woodwork, 1930s.　　　Heatherbank Museum of Social Work.

William Quarrier.

Private Children's Homes

Quarrier's Homes

William Quarrier's mother became a single parent and a working mother when his father died. In 1836, aged seven, young William worked twelve hours per day in a pin factory in Glasgow and at the age of eight he was apprenticed to a shoemaker. By the age of twenty three he had his own shoemaker's business and at New Year he regularly invited street children to a treat. There could be up to 600 children present to enjoy the feast and the magic lantern show.

In 1864 he sought and received the help of the Lord Provost of Glasgow, John Blackie, who set up a committee to consider the plight of the street children. It took too long and the slowness frustrated William Quarrier who went ahead on his own with a scheme to form boys into a Shoe-Black Brigade. He invited forty boys aged from twelve to eighteen to tea with his wife and himself at his home in Glasgow to explain his idea. The boys would work under supervision and as a team. 8d out of every 1/- earned would go to the boy. The other 4d would supply a uniform

- a cap, navy blue jacket trimmed with red braid and a red badge to be worn on the arm - and cleaning materials. They would also be taught to read and write in the evenings and at a Sabbath school.

It was the attendance at this Sunday school which caused William Quarrier to face accusations that he was stealing children from the Roman Catholic Church and trying to convert them to Protestantism. Around 50% of the boys were Catholic. He then arranged with their priests that a record of their attendance at their own church should be kept. Since education was also given to them at his school, however, many boys still opted to attend Quarrier's Sabbath School.

City Orphan Home.

David Grey

He was a wild boy who cursed and swore. He pawned his clothes so that he could gamble and lived rough. At fifteen years of age he joined the Shoe-Black Brigade promising to abandon gambling and he did so. He took a pride in his work and became the best boot brusher in Glasgow

which helped him to earn about 30/- per week. In 1865 he went to sea and yet he always kept in touch with the Quarriers, bringing them souvenirs from the countries which he visited. Unfortunately he died a few years later while on a voyage.

> Weel grannie, there was nae
> tobacco to spin
> This morn whaur I howpt a bit
> trifle to win,
> And the bobbies hae cried doun
> the match-sellin trade,
> An little at horse-haudin is to be
> made.
> Sae I wi' vexation could gruttin
> ootricht
> To think I should bring ye nae
> bawbees the nicht,
> Wheh 'twas my good luck to
> meet Jamie Dillap
> Yon callan ye thocht aye a
> pushin' wee chap.
>
> "Man, Dawnie," cried Jamie,
> "here's stunnin news noo
> I've juist pairted wi' Curly an'
> Sammy McClew,
> Wha bounci'ly tell me their
> fortune is made,
> For they've been taen on in the
> Shoe-Black Brigade.
> T'wad seem that some big anes
> hae meet an agreet
> To try an' tak' some o' us kids
> aff the street,

*An' mak' us shoe-blacks - an'
they're wantin' a lot -
Sae, Dawnie, let's aff to their
office like a shot."*

*Awa tae the office we skirted wi'
speed
To see an they ony mair laddies
micht need,
And the manager, seemin' to
fancy our looks,
Spak kindly; and, writin' our
names in his books,
Speered wha we balangt tae?
had e'er we done ocht?
Wi' wha, an' at what sort o'
business w'ed wrocht? -
A whulk bein answered, he'd
trust us, he said:
Syne fitted us out for the Shoe-
Black Brigade.*

Grannie Gemmill's O'e, John Young,
1866

Newspaper and Parcel Brigades

In 1866 William Quarrier set up a
Newspaper Brigade which gave work
to 100 boys; thirty of them lived in
The Industrial Brigade Home with a
superintendent and a matron
provided by William Quarrier, the
others lived with relatives or in
lodgings. Every morning they
received schooling in a large
classroom before setting out with a
canvas bag full of newspapers. Next
came a Parcel Brigade; again the
boys had a uniform, a table of
charges and a guarantee of honesty.
Their proud record was that no parcel
ever went missing.

Home for Destitute Children

In 1871 William Quarrier became
convinced of the need to open a
home for children in need. He had
already established a Children's Night
Asylum and in 1870 over 1,000
children had spent the maximum
time of three nights each there. His
idea was to set up a safe Christian
home for orphans or neglected
children and he asked for
subscriptions to help to buy premises.
These were found at Renfrew Lane,
Glasgow and on 18th November 1871
the first child arrived. A second home
for girls was opened nearby and both
were soon filled to capacity.

*Andrew came in from the
winter's rain with bare feet, and
without a jacket...dripping
wet...he looked around and
asked if there were "ony mair".
There was a warm fire. He was
stripped, washed, given clean
clothes, fed and was soon asleep
in his hammock slung from the
ceiling in the dormitory which
had bright religious texts around
the walls. Willie was next a day
or two later. His clothes were
verminous. His attitude hard
and defiant. He had committed
crimes but he was welcomed.
Jimmy was eight years old. His
mother and father were both
dead and an uncle and aunt
neglected him. He sold matches
for a living or tumbled in the
street. He slept on a stair
landing and begged scraps from
the matron at a Corbett Feeding
Station. It was she who brought
him to Quarrier's.*

Adapted from *The Life Story of William
Quarrier*, J. Urquhart, 1900

City Orphan Homes

The City Orphan Homes opened
houses at Cessnock House, Govan in
1872, with its spaciousness and
gardens where swings and a
playground could be provided. Next
came Elmpark for girls. Boys and
girls with many different but
harrowing stories were admitted.
Many were abandoned, others were
on the edge of sinking down into a
life of crime. Sarah was six and was
kept locked up all day in a room by
herself. Maggie sold newspapers to
make pennies to buy food. Her father
was killed in a building accident. The
homes became so popular that
sometimes children would forge
stories that they were orphans or
deserted to be taken in. Each case
was investigated and those who told
lies were usually found out.

At last in 1877 Quarrier's dream
of a village with family homes came
true when the Bridge of Weir Cottage
Homes were opened. Each villa had
its 'father and mother' a couple who
cared for thirty boys and girls of all
ages and moulded them into a large

family. Each 'father' had to have a
trade which he could teach. By 1890
there was a school, a hall, a church
with seating for 800, an Invalid Home
with forty beds, a sanatorium, a farm
and workshops and a model ship, the
James Arthur where thirty boys were
taught seamanship. There was also a
seaside Home at Ardnadam, Dunoon.

In 1890 there were 1,200
children who came from many parts
of Scotland. 700 from Glasgow, 150
from Edinburgh, 80 from
Renfrewshire, others from Stirling,
Aberdeen, Tilliecoultry, Alloa and
Stornoway.

Emigration

The schemes which were in place to
send orphans and other children to
Canada and Australia were looked
upon as giving them a new start in
life and went on as late as the 1960s.
The idea came from a London
philanthropist, Maria Rye, who
bought an old jail on the shores of
Lake Ontario in 1868, and brought
sixty eight children from London and
Liverpool, housed them in this centre
and advertised them for adoption or
as trainee farmhands and servants.
Annie Macpherson, a Scot working as
a 'social worker' in London, was
impressed by Rye's work and in the
1870s she founded a distribution
home at Lake Ontario and organised
one hundred boys to be sent out to
Canada. Some were adopted not
hired.

When William Quarrier met Miss
Annie Macpherson he felt that this
scheme was the answer to break 'the
chain of street begging, reformatory,
penitentiary and the grave.' He saw
this as an opportunity to 'deprive the
poorhouse of as many children as
possible.' He and others believed that
it was a 'golden opportunity for a
new life'. The children were not
compelled to go and permission was
sought from relatives if possible.

*We who labour here are tired of
relieving misery from hand to
mouth, and also heartsick of
seeing hundreds of families
pining away for want of work,
when over on the shores of
Ontario, the cry is heard, "Come
over and we will help you."...give*

us the power to make a golden bridge across the Atlantic.

Annie MacPherson, 1869

Going to a better land, was how the idea was presented to the children. They lined up in procession led by the biggest boys, with the toddlers at the rear. The youngest was three years old and was called Danny. He knew he was going to Canada but he did not understand where it was or why he should go there.

Two of the first batch were not orphans and had parents who came to see them off. Jim, whose father was paralysed and could not cope, and Charlie, eight years old, whose father was dying. Unsuccessful attempts had been made to have Bella and Nellie adopted together in Scotland and now the sisters were bound for Canada. Bella sat hugging her doll. In Canada she took cholera and died.

Maggie sang at fairs at Kilmarnock and Ayr. There were only two songs which she knew but she had big eyes and sang with pathos *Driven from Home* and *Far, Far at Sea*. She had been sleeping on stairs in Glasgow until someone let her sleep under their bed. The cost per head was £10 and the money came from donations.

Each boy was given a Bible, a copy of John Bunyan's *The Pilgrim's Progress*, a purse and a pocket knife. They also received 2 linen suits, 1 cloth suit, 4 shirts, 4 pairs of socks - provided by the ladies of the Dorcas Society - a box of collars, a pair of boots, a writing case and a Band of Hope pledge card. These were placed in a strong wooden chest. The children went to receiving homes and then were sent to farms to live with Canadian families. The Rev Edward Stobo wrote:

My Dear Friend,

In this country the servant sits at the table with the family, and what a table! - say breakfast. There on the nice, neatly spread white cloth, is laid out a large dish of mush, fried bacon, boiled green corn, potatoes, bread, stewed and raw raspber-

ries or cherries, cucumbers, tomatoes, honey, doughnuts, ginger snaps ... such a change for our poor street children. Here the little ones have a chance for life.

Adapted from *The Life Story of William Quarrier*, J. Urquhart, 1900

William Quarrier set up his own receiving home in Brockville, Province of Ontario, in 1881. The scheme was halted for some years in 1897 but resumed in 1904 after his death. After 1928 it was illegal to send a child under fourteen abroad without an adult but until the 1960s children over fourteen were still sent away.

However, in recent years evidence has been gathered which tells some horrific stories of mistreatment, abuse and exploitation and isolation of these children especially in Australia. Proper records were not always kept and some were destroyed. Several children had parents who for some reason could not cope and placed them temporarily, as they thought, in a home only to discover when their circumstances changed that they could find no information as to their whereabouts.

Even in 1872, as the first party of sixty four boys and girls from Quarrier's were setting out for Canada doubts were expressed by some people but these were mainly bemoaning the fact that the children were a loss to the labour market. Pouring our slum children abroad was bringing trouble to Canada, according to one Edinburgh lady. The *Glasgow Herald* was sceptical and several articles and letters were published against the practice.

Farm schools abroad

Orphans and destitute children were placed in farm schools from 1916 onwards at Vancouver Island, Canada and Fairbridge, Australia, 'where they live under specially happy conditions.'

This latter school has recently come in for fierce criticism and cases of abuse have come to light, chronicled in *Empty Cradles* by

Margaret Humphries published by the Child Migrant Trust. The Scottish Council for Women's Trades made the initial selection believing that this was the best solution for those children. Recent investigations have discovered that cruelty and abuse were rife and that great mental and physical suffering was often the lot of these boys.

Cruelty

Children's Aid Society

The Edinburgh and Leith Children's Aid and Refuge Society was founded in 1877 by Miss Emma Stirling. Later the national Children's Aid Society opened nurseries to which mothers could bring their pre-school children while they themselves went to work. On arrival each child was bathed and put into clothes belonging to the institution then fed breakfast, lunch and spent the day playing before being dressed in their own clothes to be taken home at night. The cost was 2d per day and they were run voluntarily by a committee of ladies.

The Scottish Society for the Prevention of Cruelty to Children

James Grahame visited a circus in Glasgow at Christmas in 1878 and was shocked by the treatment of a boy of four years of age by an acrobat. He reported this to the Chief Constable but as the contortionist had moved on to Manchester nothing could be done. On a visit to New York, in 1881, he read about an acrobat being prosecuted for cruelty. It was the same man and boy. The man had used a red-hot poker to force the child to learn new tricks. In New York James Grahame discovered a Children's Shelter run by the New York Society for the Prevention of Cruelty to Children which had opened there in 1874.

He attempted to form a Society in Glasgow, in 1878, but people would not believe that such cruelty existed. Eventually, in July 1884, he succeeded and an office and shelter was opened. 595 cases involving 1,173 children were dealt with in its first year. In October 1884 a similar Society opened in Edinburgh. They joined forces with the original Children's Aid Societies and became known, in 1889, as The Scottish National Society for the Prevention of Cruelty to Children, more commonly called The Cruelty.

The Cruelty Men

From an original force of three a band of inspectors now operated throughout Scotland. They were called the cruelty men and were considered more approachable than the police. In 1894 there were 1,843 cases of alleged cruelty involving 3,932 children dealt with by them and in 182 cases the parents were prosecuted and convicted. In 1910, 7,677 cases were investigated involving 23,140 children .

In 1901 an inspector reported that a boy of fourteen, whose parents were dead, had been found sleeping in an unoccupied house in Kerr's Close, Forres. He was destitute and covered with vermin. He had been sleeping in stables and outhouses for months. The boy was sent by the Society to the Industrial Brigade in Edinburgh. Complaints ranged from neglect, starvation (a boy shut up in a coal-hole with nothing to eat), mental cruelty (a child forced by foster parents to sit in a cold bath for hours), and brutality (beating by a drunken father); other children were simply abandoned.

Murrayfield Home

In 1889 a Children's Home and shelter was opened in Edinburgh to cope with children removed from the custody of their parents. The children attended the nearest school and a Sunday School was held at the Home. For those too young for school there was a nursery with rocking horses and a doll's house.

During the year seven boys have been sent to work. Four as page-boys, two apprenticed to trades and one as a shop message-boy. Three have been admitted to the Industrial Brigade [Quarrier's]. Two girls have been sent to

service...In the summer vacation the bigger boys worked at a neighbouring dairy and market garden.

Annual Report, S.N.S.P.C.C., 1891

After the Prevention of Cruelty to Children Act 1894 was passed the Scottish Society became the Scottish Branch of the National Society and did not regain independence until 1907. In 1921 the accolade of 'Royal' was added to its name in recognition of the work carried out over thirty seven years.

Funding

The Society was supported entirely by subscriptions and voluntary contributions, although some legacies and large donations helped. The Workmen's Fund, subscriptions collected every week from men at factories, mills and shipyards, was also appreciated. In 1897 there were twenty five Lady Collectors in Glasgow and 111 in Edinburgh. Each collected from the homes of ordinary people in her area who gave a stated sum per month - by 1910 there were 758 collectors in sixty five districts throughout Scotland and a house to house and street collection was held on Heather Day every year to raise funds.

Prevention of Cruelty to Children Act 1894

Under this Act parents or guardians could not permit boys under fourteen or girls under sixteen to beg, sell, sing, play or perform in the street for gain. No children were to be admitted to licensed premises to entertain between the hours of 9pm and 6am and no childen under eleven allowed to perform on licensed premises at any time. No children under sixteen were to be trained as acrobats unless it was one of their parents who carried out the training. However a School Board could grant a licence which permitted a child over seven to be employed in public entertainment or acrobatic training provided that they were satisfied as to their fitness and that provision was made for their health and that they were treated kindly.

Children's League of Pity

This was the junior wing of the Scottish National Society for the Prevention of Cruelty to Children. The Marchioness of Tweedsdale and her daughter, Lady Clementine Hay, founded it in 1893 to encourage children to learn about those less well provided for. The magazine of the League was called *City Sparrows* and members were asked to donate their pennies.

You children, who have as yet done nothing for them [the 6,000 children helped in 1896] can now help us to reach them if you will, that we may reform the bad homes and give again to the children the gracious gift of childhood of which they have been robbed.

City Sparrows, Jubilee edition, 1897

Corbett Cooking Depots

Thomas Corbett moved to London but was originally from Glasgow. In the 1880s he gave money to set up cooking depots where a meal could be bought for less than 6d. Many children were so poor that they could not even afford that and lived off the left over scraps from these depots.

Poor Children's Dinner Table Society

This was first considered in 1868 to ensure that needy children whose families were too poor to provide for them were given a hot meal daily. The first Table opened in Glasgow, in February 1869. Three lady visitors were employed who examined each case individually in detail to decide if the child qualified when a ticket was issued which entitled the child to attend daily at the nearest Table. During the winter 1900-1901, 190,402 dinners were served at the fourteen Tables which were set up in halls close to schools and opened at 12.30pm every weekday.

In twelve different districts a table is spread on five days of the week. Each table is presided over by two ladies. The dinner consisting of soup and bread, is brought from a central depot, and about twelve o'clock each day there may be seen converging towards these centres of attraction a large number of hungry children of all ages and conditions. Tickets admitting the children have previously been distributed by agents of the society, and a supply is always in the hands of the School Board Officers who have discretionary power to send any hungry or destitute child once to these tables, and as this not only supplies a meal, but, as the name and address are written on the ticket, brings the child to the notice of the superintendents and in many cases clothing or boots and shoes are provided. A look-out is kept that the children are attending school, and thus a double end is served.

William Mitchell, Vice Chairman of the School Board, *Good Words*, June 1886

Children's Day Refuges

These were set up by the Evangelistic Association to provide a free Sunday dinner for children. The next step was to offer weekday refuges where, after due investigation of financial means by a visit to their family by an officer of the Association, the children were admitted daily to the church Mission Hall. The morning began with family worship, then a substantial breakfast of porridge and milk was served and the children marched to the nearest Board School and returned for a dinner of soup and bread. After school there was a Bible lesson and a supper of porridge and milk. They were sent home at 6.30pm.

Feeding centres

The Scottish Trades Union Congress in 1898 advocated free meals for schoolchildren and re-inforced the demand again in 1905 and 1907 that the School Board should be responsible for the cost and not the Parish Council, as was being proposed in the Education (Scotland) Bill 1908. Education authorities did set up feeding centres on the enactment of this legislation and under the Education (Scotland) Act 1918 . Up until 1924 meals were provided for mothers and children recommended to the local authorities by the Child Welfare Services. The charge per meal was around 4d.

During the miners' strike in the Fife coalfield in November 1920 the Education Department provided three meals per day to all school children. Non-school children were fed with meal, bread, butter, kippers and sausages paid for weekly by a grant from the Town Council.

Soup kitchens

During the 1926 miners' strike every miners' row had its own soup kitchen. At Cowie the food was served in a hut at the school. The children were given a plate of soup then chose which queue to join for either bread and butter or bread and jam.

Soup kitchen, 1930. East Dunbartonshire Libraries.

It was in the wash-house, a huge boiler and they lit the fire underneath the water and my father would clean rabbits, cut them all up, or hares and put them all into the big boiler with the water...they [the miners] all took turns at bringing a bag of vegetables, from their gardens, for the soup.

Stirling Oral History Project, miner's daughter, Cowie, 1926

Grey Lodge Settlement

Mary Lily Walker, the first superintendent of the Dundee Social Union, in 1906 provided meals for mothers and children. During the strike at Lochee Mill in 1911, 900 mothers and their children were fed for nine days at a cost of £21.15/-.

Glasgow City Mission

This Mission was opened by David Naismith in 1826 as an inter-denominational Christian agency to help the poor. Five of the initial eight lay missionaries could speak Gaelic which was welcomed by the great number who had flocked from the Highlands in search of work. They also started a school for chimney sweeps as many boys were put to this work so young that they did not receive any education. Around thirty boys were helped each year. By 1859 it employed fifty seven missionaries feeding, clothing, educating and training children and young people.

Boarding Institutions

The Glasgow Institution for Orphan and Destitute Girls

This society was established in 1826 to provide a Home for orphans or poor girls who had no support. It was stressed in the Annual Report of 1882 that the Home was not a reformatory. One girl that year was admitted because her mother was 'in the poorhouse, hopelessly insane'. On admission each girl was provided, by the member of the Ladies Committee who supported her application, with 3 chemises, 2 night gowns, 6 pocket handkerchiefs, 2 flannel and 2 coloured petticoats, 1 Sunday frock, 2 house frocks, 1 jacket or cloak, 1 hat, 2 pairs of shoes, 1 pair of slippers, 3 pairs of stockings, a brush and comb and an umbrella.

The Home was supervised by a matron and run by a committee of ladies most of whom lived at 'good' addresses in the West End of the city. Mrs John Colville of Helensburgh and Mrs Vernon of Mugdock Castle, members of the Ladies Committee, would invite the girls to their home for a day. There was also a holiday home at Kirn. In 1882 there were seventy 'little homeless and motherless' girls. At New Year the Home was given, amongst other donations, moral tracts, an entertainment - usually a magic lantern show, a barrel of apples, a web of serge, a web of wincyette. Miss Kerr gifted thirty new trimmed hats, gloves, ribbons, knitted cuffs, cakes and Christmas pies.

In 1891 a new Home at Whiteinch was opened free of debt, owing to generous legacies and donations, without there having to be a public appeal. There was accommodation for sixty girls who attended the nearest elementary board school for their education. The girls were trained in housework for one year, after Standard 6 at school, to make them suitable for domestic service and no girl was allowed to leave the Home until a place of work in a suitable house was found for her. A member of the Ladies Committee visited her at her workplace every week and reported to the Committee.

Perth Ladies' House of Refuge for Destitute Girls

The aims of the Perth Ladies' House of Refuge, opened on 23rd May 1844, were to ensure a good elementary education combined with religious instruction for girls whose parents failed to provide for them. The matron appointed must endeavour, 'by her whole walk and conversation, to induce them savingly to embrace the great truths of Christianity.' The girls, from ten to fourteen years of age, were orphans or else neglected or in moral danger.

A number of ladies volunteered to act as visitors whose job was to vet enquiries for application and to take their turn to inspect the Home weekly. They were often shocked at the conditions under which many children lived as their reports show:

A   *Eleven years old; father dead; mother alive, and a very wicked woman; only married once; has three children since husband's death; has been in jail for stealing; receives 3/- a week, with which to support a family of five.*

B   *Twelve years old; father and mother alive; mother a drunkard; wicked woman; teaches B- to steal; beats her if she refuses; B- a well-disposed girl.*

C   *Twelve years old; father dead; mother alive and in great poverty; is a drunkard; sister a prostitute.*

First Report, Perth Ladies' House of Refuge, 1845

The matron, Mrs McNab, reported an improvement in the behaviour of most of the girls under her care within a year. They were orderly, steady and obliging in the house, quiet in their deportment on the street and correct in their behaviour during Divine worship. The girls learned sewing and knitting and their work was sold yielding a profit of £2.5.8d in the first year.

Dennistoun Children's Refuge

The Archbishop of Glasgow founded this institution as a temporary shelter for children who were in moral danger. It opened in Whitevale Street, Dennistoun on 2nd February 1887, under the charge of an all male committee and the Sisters of Charity, who staffed it.

In 1901, after fifteen years in existence the Refuge had admitted 2,600 children who stayed at the refuge from one day to one year and a few for a longer period. In a report of 1901 the committee experienced delight that many had been either returned to their families, whose financial situation had improved to enable them to once again provide for their children, placed in Catholic families or found work in domestic service, adopted, admitted into Lady

Children admitted				
Age	1898	1899	1900	1901
Under 6	43	59	61	51
6 - 9	47	50	59	43
9 - 11	28	22	35	14
over 11	30	23	21	18

Bute's Institutions or Smyllum Orphanage, Lanark, boarded out with foster parents or placed under Catholic guardianship by admission into Industrial Schools. Four are recorded, between 1898 and 1901, as having died.

Any sign of infectious disease and the Sisters had the child removed to hospital. In the summer months the children were taken to stay in a house rented by the Sisters of Charity in Girvan. The committee employed an Outdoor Officer who assessed the children and decided the best plan for their welfare. Several children who had been in the Refuge for a longer period were boarded out under the Poor Law Act of 1897.

Monetary support came from contributions from the various missions, public works, companies, private donations, Celtic Football Club and the League of the Cross Billiards Society, all of whom gave generously in kind as well. Mr Bilsland, the baker, gave baskets of pastries, jams and jellies came from Dundee and many ladies committees provided clothing.

At Christmas toys, including a rocking horse, were provided and entertainments were arranged and turkeys, cakes, sweets and oranges donated.

Case histories

Three children, whose ages ranged from four to seven, were found in a house absolutely without furniture of any kind. There were only a few stale crusts of bread for the little ones... and they were all naked. They were in an indescribable state when admitted to the Refuge... Both parents had given way to drink, the mother was in prison and the father had given up all interest in the house.

Two boys, aged six and eight, were received into the Refuge in an emaciated state. The mother after a long illness had died, and the father was half-starved like his children. He too became seriously ill, developing symptoms of consumption... He died after receiving the last sacrament. The children are still at the Refuge.

Three children, ages ranging from two to six, the father, a reserveman, called to his regiment to serve in South Africa, the mother dying, living in a small house, unable to mind the children. Their friends were of a very low class and spent the allowance given by the war funds on themselves ... A member of the Soldiers and Sailors Family Association brought the little ones to the Refuge.

Report for 1898-1901,
Children's Refuge, 1901

St Vincent de Paul Society

The Society opened a Working Boys Home in Glasgow in 1897. It provided accommodation for older boys who were earning a wage. Similar homes were also supported by this Society in other cities in Scotland to provide a Christian environment for boys and to ensure that they were fed and kept away from temptation. They also supported day nurseries and opened a convalescent and holiday home at Langbank where Roman Catholic children, aged five to twelve years were cared for free of cost.

Invalid Children's Aid Association

This Association had homes at St Andrews, Clynder and Strathblane where children could convalesce. The Dundee branch bought a holiday home at Auchterhouse . They also provided accommodation for healthy children for short periods if their parents were ill and gave help and advice to families with physically or mentally handicapped children.

Kindergarten

In November 1906 in Edinburgh Lilleen Hardy opened St Saviour's Child-Garden with three children in her care. 'The Wummin' had to learn a new language as her way of speaking was strange to her young charges. The 'fit o' the press' was the bottom of the cupboard; 'screw the well' - turn on the tap; always 'What's wrong?' never what is the matter?; as well as coos, wurrums, dugs and cuddies - cows, worms, dogs and horses.

From twelve children from three to five years old the nursery grew and trust was built up within the community. It became known as the 'Good Morning School'! The children attended from 9.30am - 12.30pm every day. On arrival they hung their outdoor things on their own peg and put on blue overalls with red collars and cuffs. Hands and faces were inspected and it became a disgrace to be sent to wash at school. Fathers began to take an interest and one gifted a canary, another a goldfish, while one made a barrow. A mother made a big rag doll which they called Mary. They soon learned discipline and one little girl told another, 'the beads are no' fur keepin'. Sometimes children were absent because 'ma shoes were at the mendin' or they were 'lettin' in'.

Nannie, in 1909, was described as having 'nae hat, nae coat, nae shoes, nae stockins, nae drawers and nae frock'. She was sent out in the same goonie which she wore day and night. Then one day she found a green straw hat with green ribbons and could not be parted from it.

The Good Morning School, Lileen Hardy, 1912

Country week

In July, nine children, between three and five years old, arrived at the tram stop complete with paper parcels. All the boots had new laces and mothers had done their best to turn the children out smart. They were off to Portobello for a week. They had a wonderful time playing at cuddies - one jumping on the other one's back - and being carried across the sand, making sand castles and paddling.

Glasgow Day Nurseries Association

This Association was founded in 1883 to provide a safe place for working mothers to leave their children. When the first six creches were opened they catered for around 200 children from babies to two years of age. In 1917 those children from three to five attended what became known as kindergartens. These were open from 7.30am-5pm and Dr Sutherland in his report for 1918 remarks that mostly the children's mothers were charwomen as the hours were unsuitable for factory workers. During World War One, although most children attended daily, a few were admitted as boarders from Monday to Friday. These were the children of munition workers.

The lack of space for playing out-of-doors was seen as a drawback and voluntary workers took the children to the nearest park for fresh air.

Children should have the use of school playgrounds, gardens and playrooms with toys.

The Children of the City, James Russell, 1886

Some people, however, felt that nurseries were breeding grounds for infectious disease. This was not borne out by statistics which showed that children attending them were usually taller, heavier and brighter than average. Where possible parents contributed towards their child's upkeep. A meal was provided daily by the Cosy Corner Restaurant.

Country homes

Children suffering from malnutrition or rickets were sent to country homes run by the local authorities to benefit from fresh air and good wholesome food. In 1925 children about to be sent to such a home for a break were isolated for a week for observation to ensure that they carried no vermin, skin or infectious disease and a reception house was set up for this purpose.

During World War One a Country Home for Toddlers was set up at

Lochgoilhead under the Glasgow Infant Health Visitors Association and staffed by Girl Guide officers. An eight apartment cottage was rented as a children's home at Auchencairn, Kirkcudbright by Old Kilpatrick Parish Council in 1913 as it was considered that the maintenance cost of 5/- per child was cheaper than keeping them in their poorhouse.

Fresh Air Fortnight Scheme

The Glasgow Evangelistic Association, the Poor Children's Fresh Air Fortnight and Crippled Children's League set up homes, from 1886 onwards, in Roberton, Balmaha, Cove, Maybole, Prestwick and Saltcoats. They also arranged accommodation in farmhouses, school houses, cottages and inns in the country and seaside to give two weeks holiday to needy and feeble children who lived in slum areas and who rarely breathed fresh air. The funds were voluntarily provided and the Duchess of Montrose was its active patron.

> *The Board of Management have also to acknowledge the great kindness with which the Duchess of Montrose has received, through the mediation of the Poor Children's Fresh Air Fortnight Committee and its energetic convenor, Mr MacKeith, a large number of children from the Shelter into her 'Holiday Home', to their great benefit and enjoyment during the past year.*
>
> Annual Report, Scottish Society for the Prevention of Cruelty to Children, 1894

By 1930, 273,901 children had benefitted from the scheme.

Holiday colonies

Holidays in farmhouses, schoolhouses and country inns were arranged for groups of primary children aged seven years and upwards who were recommended by their head teachers as in need of a break. Older children, up to fourteen years of age, were sometimes included in the scheme.

Clothing exchange, Clydebank.   West Dunbartonshire Libraries.

Island of Shuna

Mr Yates, the owner, bequeathed the island of Shuna to the City of Glasgow in 1891 and proposed it be used as a summer resort for 'feeble folk', young and old, in need of a change of air during a longer period than a fortnight.

Depression - 1930s

A deputation of seven Clydebank mothers representing various organisations, of all shades of political opinion, waited for over two hours in the lobby of the Education Committee Headquarters in Park Circus, Glasgow, on Wednesday afternoon, November 2nd 1933, before being admitted to plead for better provision of boots and clothing to the school children of the unemployed in the Burgh. There was a disagreement amongst the Committee Members as to whether the deputation should be heard or not. By a large majority it was decided to listen to their case.

The mothers were asking for one suit, under-clothing, one pair of boots and two pairs of stockings, the boots to be offered twice per year to the children of the unemployed. The relief scale for a man with a wife and six children was 38/- per week, but after paying out rent, light and

heat they only had 13/6 left to feed and clothe their children.

Clydebank Press, November, 1933

Distress funds

In 1908 the Bootless Children's Fund was set up to help the children of the unemployed to ensure that they had boots or shoes to see them through the winter. During the Depression of the 1930s this organisation again was put in place and other distress funds were set up to organise clothing and food. These came about because the sight of shivering children coming into police stations begging for a ticket to obtain food from the soup kitchens upset the police officers who often paid out money from their own pockets when the supply of tickets was finished so that children would not starve. Many organisations ran concerts to raise money for the funds.

Clothing exchanges

The provision of clothing exchanges was also of great benefit. Equivalent to the modern Nearly New Shops, these were run by volunteers, often from the Women's Voluntary Association. Clothes which older children had outgrown were gladly seized upon by mothers of younger children. They were usually set up in town halls or other council property.

Parish clothes

The post of Public Assistance Officer was created and part of the remit was to oversee the provision of clothing for school children of parents in receipt of benefit. A grant of £6 was given to foster parents of boarded out children.

Parish clothes were distinctive and considered a mark of shame and most families tried to avoid being dressed by the parish. So that the garments could not be pawned or resold they were marked with indelible ink. They were usually one size too big to allow for growth. Sometimes local authorities would make an arrangement with the Co-operative Society or other clothier whereby vouchers were given out to be redeemed against clothing. Although this might ensure the correct fit there was a limited selection offered for each item and these were not the ordinary garments sold but ones produced for the parish. Boys were given heavy, rough tweed, herring-bone suits and girls received navy serge gym slips and black stockings.

Poor Children's Clothing Guild

The Glasgow Academy Sewing Meeting, branches of Voluntary Visitors, work parties in churches and schools, Dorcas Society and Zenana Society members made clothing for children whose parents were too poor to provide for them but were not on the Poor Law Register. When this function was taken over by the education authority in 1924 the focus changed to provision for very young children and maternity bundles were distributed through the Departments of Child Welfare to those in need.

Midgey rakers

During the Depression children would raid the bins in the middens of people living in better off areas in search of cast-off clothing or anything which could be sold or pawned to bring in a few pennies.

Treat

The Glasgow Charles Dickens Society provided its first treat for children from the slums of the city in 1906. In 1934, it entertained 1,200 needy children at the St Andrew's Hall giving them a Christmas dinner and gifts.

Education of the blind

Since 1793 there had been a Blind Asylum in Edinburgh and under the Poor Law of 1860 blind pauper children were to be educated by right. Home teachers were introduced before this date. They helped the children cope with learning braille by leaving them books from the Free Library of the Mission to the Outdoor Blind. Because of locational difficulties there were often long gaps between visits making it difficult for some children to learn. The day school was managed by fourteen directors and admitted children from six to fourteen years of age. In 1867 the Glasgow Blind Asylum also opened a day school and children whose parents could not afford the fees were admitted free of charge. Sixteen children attended in that year.

In October 1868, the teacher at the Mid Parish School, Greenock, agreed to take a blind boy into the school. He was so successful that he won first prize amongst twelve sighted children. The Directors of the Charity School, in 1869, arranged to teach five other blind children and the original boy transferred there also. Alston's raised letter in Roman capitals were used so that other seeing children could help the blind with their lessons. Braille books were not always available for every subject and ordinary books were marked so that parents could assist the child at home. A board pierced with diagonal holes, first used in the Edinburgh Blind Asylum, into which pins could be fitted, one end of the pin representing the even, the other the odd, was used to teach arithmetic. Model relief maps were used to teach geography.

Those who commenced with the ABC are now able to read the Bible intelligently.

Annual Report, Greenock Charity School, Thomas Kay, Headmaster, 1870

In 1896 the Braille Writing Association began to provide text books for use in schools.

Education of Blind and Deaf Mute Children (Scotland) Act 1890

This Act proposed that specially trained teachers should be appointed to teach blind children. It encouraged School Boards to provide for blind children by installing special equipment at selected schools, always up to Standard 2 and desirable up to Standard 5 and upwards where possible. Schools specialising in education for blind children could be boarding schools or day schools. Parents were obliged in 1918 to send their children to school. In 1926, several pupils passed the Qualifying Examination and went on to a Higher Grade School.

The Welfare of the Blind Persons Act 1920 continued the provision of education for children, some in special day schools others in residential institutions in many towns throughout Scotland: braille, knitting, beading and sewing were taught. At the age of sixteen they went on to learn mattress making, brush making, machine knitting. Boys were also taught carpet-mat making, chair covering and boot repairing. They were also employed in splitting and bunching sticks for firewood.

Of one hundred and twenty-eight children or young persons five to eighteen years of age, ninety-two are at school and fifteen are in technical training, leaving twenty-one at home or casually employed or unemployed, and for these last training in a useful handicraft is desirable. There are only two registered pre-school children and the Sisters of St Vincent [St Vincent School, Tollcross, Glasgow] tell me [A.K. Chalmers, former Medical Officer of Health] they are prepared to take children of tender years.

The Health of Glasgow, 1818-1925, An Outline, A.K. Chalmers, 1930

Education

The Industrial Revolution of the eighteenth century had resulted in overcrowded conditions in the areas where factories had spread and this was worsening all through the nineteenth century in the large manufacturing towns. By 1844 many caring people were trying to wrestle with the problems which were building up due to the change in the lives of the workforce from rural life and home industries. The first sign of that change was the rapid increase in population in small villages where factories and mills were being set up to utilise the water-driven machinery, and later the much greater movement away from the rural areas into factories in the new industrial areas which were utilising the revolutionary steam driven machinery to manufacture goods.

In Edinburgh in the winter of 1847/1848 there were 2,503 deaths from fevers. Disease, including cholera, in the mid nineteenth century had left many children either orphans, fatherless or motherless with no-one to care for them, or they had parents whose answer to their horrible living and working conditions was to drink themselves silly and were therefore not capable of looking after their families. Often these children slept rough in the wynds and closes of the large cities and begged, raked middens or stole to staunch their hunger.

Industrial schools

In 1840 it was estimated that in Aberdeen there were around 280 children begging on the streets. There were a few City Missions which tried to cope but the parochial schools refused to allow children to attend if they did not have 'suitable

Chemistry class, Hutchesons' Grammar School, 1938.

clothes'. The first day industrial school in Scotland was opened in that city in October 1841, by Sheriff William Watson, to feed and train boys in work habits and to give a basic education. Originally called an Industrial Feeding School, because basic meals were provided, at first it catered for children of eight to fourteen years of age who were exposed to moral danger through the misconduct of their parents and was not open to those convicted of crime.

The school was well supported by voluntary subscription. Because this school appeared to be successful in dealing with the problem of children, 'nurtured in ignorance, vice and crime' a female industrial school was opened in Aberdeen in 1843 and a second for boys in the same city in 1845.

The Governor of Edinburgh prison had put up a proposal for a scheme to establish a School of Industry in Edinburgh in 1842 and

the United Industrial School opened in November 1847. The number of children who passed through this school in three years was 740 and Governor John Smith was delighted at the fall in the numbers of boys being sent to prison.

Further schools were opened: Perth in 1843 had 135 boys, of whom 40 were orphans, 49 were fatherless, 15 were motherless and 31 had worthless parents. Dundee opened a similar school in 1846: there were 85 boys - 14 orphans, 39 fatherless, 17 motherless and 15 with worthless parents: there were also 55 girls in the school. In 1853 a letter from the Superintendent of Police in Dundee stated that 'it was now a rare thing to see a juvenile arraigned in the assize court.' Many other towns followed their lead. Some were single sex schools and others were mixed.

An Industrial School opened in Dumfries in 1848 and in Stirling in 1849. The children were expected to help with the domestic chores and were examined each year by the schoolmaster and the minister in their academic and religious subjects. Attendance at such schools was not compulsory but the supporters of them were convinced that they prevented children turning to crime. At the schools in Dumfries and Maxwelltown the pupils made enough profit from the sale of their work to pay for all their food. The type of work undertaken was mending fishermen's nets, making paper bags for shop keepers, picking horsehair for use in the manufacture of chairs, sofas and mattresses.

It was reported in the *Poor Law Magazine* of 1879 that these schools had reduced the number of boys sent to prison by 50%.

Juvenile commitments to prison		
Dumfries: 1847	-	40
1848	-	28
1851	-	12

The success rate was such that it was claimed that 70% of boys never re-offended. The concept behind industrial schools was to offer Christian values but not to over-educate the pupils. They were to learn discipline, moral training and basic skills which would ensure them a job of work after they left. Their maintenance was to be borne by the Parochial Board.

The first Industrial Schools (Scotland) Act 1854 permitted magistrates to commit to the schools any child under fourteen years of age found begging, not having a settled place to live, having no proper guardianship, no financial subsistence or found wandering. James Moncrieff's Education Bill, put forward in 1855, proposed that the schools should be national, non-sectarian and offer asylum to all children. This was not adopted and although many schools tried to be non-sectarian and permitted a conscience clause about religious instruction many others tended to favour one particular denomination.

In 1857 the Parochial Boards cut their poor relief support for children entering industrial schools severely

and in a further Act of 1861 funds were not to be made available for any child not committed by a magistrate. An 1866 Act allowed children up to sixteen years to be detained whether having committed an offence or not if they were needy and also the cost of their food and clothing could be paid for by the Parochial Board. Some schools provided lodgings and many of them, including the United Industrial School, Edinburgh, became boarding schools.

After 1872, parents whose children were truants and who were incapable of ensuring that they attended the parochial school were often asked by the School Board to permit them to be sent to an industrial school and unless they agreed the parents were prosecuted.

Ragged Schools

Dr Thomas Guthrie was appointed minister, in 1837, at Greyfriars Parish Church of Scotland in Edinburgh. He was born on a farm at Brechin in 1803 and had been minister at Arbirlot, Angus. Being used to the country he was appalled to see poor children, younger than five, begging on the streets. There was an Act against begging passed in 1547 but it only applied to those between the ages of fourteen and seventeen, 'whether or not there is any pretence of singing, playing, performing or offering for sale.' These children were so hungry that they raked the middens or stole food. These 'street arabs,' as they were called, if they were caught thieving and were seven years old or over were sent to prison in the infamous Tolbooth along with adults as there was no alternative.

Guthrie was a leading light in the Disruption of the Church of Scotland which saw the breaking away of many ministers to form the Free Church of Scotland. At Anstruther, the birthplace of another reformer, Thomas Chalmers, he saw a picture of a crippled shoemaker with a group of boys and girls around him teaching them his craft. Guthrie became interested in the ideas of this man, John Pounds of Portsmouth, who set up, in 1844, what he called

Ragged Schools, similar to the industrial schools but with a more religious fervour, to cater for the neglected children of that port.

Guthrie went around Edinburgh talking to the neglected children and asking them whether they would attend each day a school which would guarantee to feed them as well as teach them. One boy, Jimmy, answered, 'that an' I will, an' bring a' the land [the occupants of his tenement home] as well'.

Thomas Guthrie in 1847 published his *First Plea for Ragged Schools* which brought in sufficient funds to set up a school in Edinburgh. Donors were those who gave £5 or more and subscribers those who gave 10/- upwards. Originally he had hoped to use the large room beneath Free St John's Church but the congregation refused permission and a room was hired at Ramsay Lane, Castlehill. 50% of the original intake were Roman Catholic children although there were complaints from the Catholic clergy that it was a conspiracy to steal children from that faith and convert them. Although there was great emphasis on such matters as the catechism no child was forced to attend religious education contrary to its faith. On Sundays all children were urged to attend their own place of worship.

> *To give children an adequate allowance of food for their daily support.*
>
> *To instruct them in reading, writing and arithmetic.*
>
> *To train them in habits of industry, by instructing and employing them daily in such sorts of work as are suited to their years.*
>
> *To teach them the truths of the Gospel, making the Holy Scriptures the groundwork of instruction.*
>
> *On the Sabbath children shall receive food as on other days, and such religious instruction as shall be arranged by the Acting Committee.*
>
> *Constitution and Rules of the Association for the Establishment of Ragged Schools for Destitute Children in Edinburgh.* June 1847

Annie B. aged thirteen years was one of the earliest pupils. Brought up by an uncle who owned a lodging house she had to serve drink to his lodgers at any hour of the day or night. She was found a home with a widow and attended the Original Ragged School where she 'found her Saviour'.

> *Some time ago, [1856] opposite the Post Office in the High Street, I saw coming down the street the band of Young Raggediers belonging to Dr Guthrie's School at Ramsay Gardens. They were above thirty or forty in number and were playing 'Johnny Coup' [Cope], making the High Street resound to the shrill sound of their fifes and the roll of their drums... The boys were warmly clothed, appeared to be well fed and hearty and their cheerful, if not proud, looks, were a response to their own music.*
>
> The Sliding Scale of Life, James McLevy, 1861

At Biggar Fair, held in April 1862, it was reported that:

> *The Ragged School musical band... fifes, drums and bugles entered Biggar, on a fine spring morning, playing the march of new and better times. It was a gala day to our poor boys; their faces were radiant with delight.*
>
> Biggar and the House of Fleming, William Hunter, 1867

Dr Guthrie set up three schools in Edinburgh, a boys', a girls' and a mixed infants' for those under ten years of age. The first Annual Report states that there were 310 boys, 199 girls and 230 infants under ten years of age attending the schools. In 1852 he provided some dormitories as he found children sleeping rough, sheltering in the Police yard where, although the officers were kind to them, they only had a brick for a pillow. Other pupils were boarded out and some lived at home and attended each day. There were exclusions - no child who attended a parish school could be a pupil; parents who could afford to provide an education for their child or who already were in receipt of parochial assistance.

The children's backgrounds differed: some were orphans, some had 'worthless' parents, either alcoholics, thieves or in prison for some other crime, some had no mother or were fatherless and some were deserted by their families. Thomas Guthrie was always proud to hear about raggediers, as he called them, cutting down forests in America, herding sheep in Australia, being promoted in the army or navy or in other walks of life becoming good citizens. At his funeral in February 1873 pupils at the Original Ragged School, now housed in a splendid building on the outskirts of Edinburgh, marched in the procession singing *There is a Happy Land* as a tribute to the founder.

> *Scholars leave their homes or lodging-houses or our own dormitories, to assemble at 7am in the morning, 8am in winter. They doff their rags to march for some three yards under the invigorating, cleansing shower of a large bath...Attiring themselves in school dress they work for an hour, and then (grace being said by one of the children) sit down to a comfortable breakfast of oatmeal porridge. With a reasonable allowance for play, so many hours are spent in receiving instruction, both secular and religious ... they dine at midday; work between three and six-thirty and after another diet of oatmeal porridge, about 7pm are sent away happy... very little use is made of corporal punishment.*
>
> Autobiography, Thomas Guthrie, 1875

Unused to being treated kindly, up to 30% of pupils did run away or not attend. Dr Guthrie had rules and no pupil who ran away could return unless prepared to face a boys' court which tried deserters. The court was headed by the superintendent, a figure of authority who always wore a red coat, and the boys listened to the excuses of the accused, holding up their right hand if they thought that he was absent without good cause and therefore guilty . The punishment was determined by the boys and was up to 'twelve palmies' -

being struck on the hand with the tawse or leather strap twelve times.

The Annual Report of the Original Ragged School, 1880, records that the work carried out was not for sale but for use in the schools. The shoemaking section, with twenty four boys, repaired 901 pairs of boots and made 291 pairs. The tailoring section, with twelve boys, produced 57 tweed suits, 110 pairs of moleskin trousers, 60 mattresses, 30 caps and 70 pairs of braces. The girls made 133 dresses, 98 pinafores, 105 petticoats, 130 shifts, 52 aprons, 44 night dresses and 160 boys' shirts in addition to household linen, and carried out as well darning and mending for the schools.

As the century moved on schools called 'industrial' or 'ragged' changed in two ways: some were turned into reformatories, others enrolled children who were not paupers or at risk. At Biggar the Female Industrial School was open to all the daughters of the working-class to learn sewing, knitting, singing and the three Rs and this seems to have been the case elsewhere.

Often the products made in these schools were sold to bring in a profit which went towards the upkeep of the school. In Falkirk in 1872 superior firewood was advertised at 7/- for 100 bundles and knife boxes, stools and barrows could be obtained to order. Dr Guthrie bought Marionville on the outskirts of Edinburgh and trained boys in market gardening. The produce was used in the schools and also sold for funds.

Although many of these schools were endowed - at Fraserburgh, Miss Strachan of Cortes opened the Female Industrial School in 1863 which she had had built as a memorial to her brother Dr James Strachan, Inspector of Army General Hospitals, Madras, India, while the Duke of Montrose donated the money for a School of Industry at Drymen and although a Government grant was paid much of the funding came from voluntary subscription and from fetes and bazaars which were held by the 'Ladies Committees' to raise money to defray the daily expenses. In 1869 the Sunday or Ragged School Act exempted 'philanthropic effort' from taxation.

Elementary schools

The parochial system of elementary education, (the name primary did not exist until 1901) which taught about 70% of Scottish children from the age

master for the education of the children of their parish. As the eighteenth century progressed and particularly during the nineteenth century, such provision proved increasingly difficult to achieve. Indeed many heritors were reluctant to see money spent on 'the rascal multitude' and neglected their obligation..

poor, either to build a schoolhouse or support a teacher... the low wages of many workmen [encourage them] *to be careless about their children. But perhaps the most prolific source of evil is the wages which the children at an early period can gain...The children of miners, nailers, and spinners, are most exposed to this evil, nor can it be repaired by their attendance either at weekday evening or Sabbath evening schools.*

The New Statistical Account, Parish of St Ninian's, 1841

The education in the manufacturing villages is sadly defective. This arises solely from want, not of will, but of the means on the part of the parents to educate their children. Nothing can exceed the anxiety of the parents in this respect, but they can neither spare their children's work nor their wages.

Dr Norman Macleod, speaking at Darvel in 1842

1. Domestic science class. 2. Physical education c.1916. 3. Stepped classroom, early 1900s. 4. Schoolboys, Lairdsland School, Kirkintilloch, 1900. East Dunbartonshire Libraries.

of five to thirteen, or at least for part of that time, to read, write and count and gave many the opportunity to go on to higher education, if they could afford it, was in a state of collapse by 1844 and unable to cope with the momentous changes brought about by the demands of the shifting population.

All parish schools charged fees and, however small, these could account for a large slice of a wage if there were several children to educate. There were usually free places for the children of paupers and some schools were charity schools.

Since 1541 local kirk sessions of the Church of Scotland were responsible for the parochial schools. The Church consistently believed that all children had a right to learn the three Rs. The Education Act of 1696, moreover, required landowners, as heritors of the Church, to provide a school, schoolhouse and salary for a

Some heritors wanted to suppress schools because their servants were being taught to read and write and as a result were less obedient and dutiful than when they had no education. Others, however, disagreed and believed that Scottish servants were more moral and committed fewer crimes than those who remained ignorant, especially those south of the border.

In some areas several schools were needed in a parish, which often covered a number of villages and small towns miles apart. Children might have to walk long distances to school and back, often barefoot, in all weather. In certain parts the inhabitants collected subscriptions for setting up and maintaining a school. In Fortrose in 1791 fifty guineas bought the hereditary right to present a free scholar and for twenty guineas a free scholar during the subscriber's lifetime.

The people are too few and too

Highlands and Islands

The Scottish Society in Scotland for Propagating Christian Knowledge was formed in 1704 and established several schools in the Highlands. In 1824 the Committee of Education of the General Assembly of the Church of Scotland opened schools, especially in the Highlands and Islands, which had resisted the adoption of presbyterianism.

A child attending one of these schools began and ended the day with prayers; each Saturday he or she had to learn a passage of scripture or verses of a psalm or paraphrase which must be memorised to be tested the following Monday. The Shorter Catechism was taught for an hour each day and pupils were examined regularly. They were expected to be able to answer such questions as - 'What is the chief end of man?' - and were punished if unable to do so. Six hours were spent at school each day in summer, four or five in winter and three hours on a Saturday morning. If a pupil had to walk several miles to school and back over the week they covered many miles.

Tutors

"We keep a tutor." said the herd's wife of Curlywee, as calmly as if she were a duchess... "there's mair hooses in this neighbourhood than ye wad think...Weel in simmertime, whan the colleges gang doon, we get yin o' the college lads to come...an' they pit up for fower weeks here an' three weeks there an' the bairns travel to whaur the student lad is bidin' an' gets their learnin'...we send him awa weel buskit wi' muirland claith, an' weel providit wi' butter an' eggs, oatmeal an' cheese... an' ten or twal pounds in his pooch."

The Stickit Minister, S. R. Crockett, 1895

Tutors were more usually employed by the aristocracy or the wealthier middle class families.

Adventure schools

The 'adventure' in adventure schools did not describe the type of education offered but the fact that the owner risked their own money in setting up such a school. Many were highly successful; some were called 'dame' schools, because they were opened by needy widows and often taught sewing as well as the three Rs. They were often held in a room in a small house. The first school in what became Clydebank was set up in a tenement house at 13 Tamson's Buildings, by a Mrs Pitblado, in 1871.

This private enterprise was looked on favourably by every town and village until 1715 when a tax was imposed on towns for their grammar school and immediately the adventure schools were under attack. It was the elders in individual parishes of the Church of Scotland who had the duty of warning the teacher to close the school. In the Strathendrick district, in 1715, Jean Kilpatrick privately taught sewing and darning to girls and also taught them the alphabet. She was

threatened that unless this latter activity was stopped she would be taken to court.

Endowed schools

In many areas elementary schools were gifted to the community by philanthropists who also left money for their upkeep. When these schools were given into the care of School Boards, in 1872, the value of the endowments was £80,000.

Works and colliery schools

Another form of endowed school was that set up by the owner of a factory or coal mine. In 1799, Robert Owen, considered a pioneer of education for young people, employed orphans and pauper children in his mills at New Lanark, as well as the children of his adult workers. He worked those over ten years old for thirteen hours per day then expected them to attend evening school for a further two hours. These conditions were good compared to many employers.

Annie McLeod

I could have stayed at school until I was twelve. Mr Owen would have liked that, but we needed the money, so I left on my tenth birthday [1820] and went to work. School is great fun. Once you're six you're taught upstairs in the new school.

Annie McLeod's Story, New Lanark Conservation Trust, 1993

Eglinton Iron Works in Kilwinning, Baird of Gartsherrie, Carron Iron Works, William Gillespie's Cotton Works, Glasgow, James Finlay's Cotton Works, Balfron and many more had schools and allowed time for schooling but there are many descriptions of children falling asleep at school because they had worked long hours before their release. As late as 1900 half-timers, as the children were called, worked in the Barrhead Dye Works for six hours and attended school for the rest of the day. Their hands were stained with dye and they were always very

tired. The school fees were often docked from their wages. The schoolmaster received accommodation and a salary from the company.

The parents in too many cases...send their children to be draw-boys or mill boys, or even weavers, at an age when they should be properly employed at school.

The Second Statistical Account, Parish of Balfron, 1841

There were colliery schools at Shotts, Bannockburn, Redding and Slammanan; the Earl of Mar set one up in Alloa; William Baird and Co. opened a school at Drumglass in 1871 and there were many others.

The Disruption of 1843 saw a break away of many congregations from the Church of Scotland to form the Free Church of Scotland. The latter often set up its own schools so that people had a choice, but these were based on sectarianism and rivalry rather than a genuine interest in solving the problems. There were 657 Free Church schools with 16,000 pupils by 1870.

Higher education

Endowed schools

There was no provision for higher education for the public schoolchild before 1872 unless they won one of the many bursaries which were on offer throughout Scotland. A pupil who had got on in the world, often by going to work in England or abroad, might show his appreciation to the elementary school in the village or town of his birth by either gifting while still alive or else leaving instructions in his will that capital should be invested and the interest on this used to provide a scholarship or bursary for a boy pupil of that school to further his education.

Many schools were set up throughout the country to provide a higher grade education for the poor or indigent, lacking the necessities of life. Sometimes these were the children of formerly thrifty merchants or craftsmen who had died or fallen on hard times. There were often stipulations attached, such as preference being given to those sharing a surname with the donor or whose father followed a particular craft. The Trades Houses also supported endowed schools. Dorward's Seminary in Montrose being one which was opened in 1833. Girls were also provided for in some areas.

Hutchesons' Grammar School

In 1639 George and Thomas Hutcheson of Lambhill, Glasgow, set up a mortification - the action of giving lands or money for charitable purposes - to provide a hospital - a place of refuge - for the poor of their surname. A part of the funds was set aside to provide maintenance, clothing and education for a number of boys who were the sons of burgesses. In the eighteenth century those receiving charity from Blair's or Baxter's mortifications could also attend this school. By 1816 the school had eighty boys receiving instruction for four years in reading, writing, arithmetic, English grammar and church music. There were twenty one boys admitted each year.

The burgess ticket of the boy's father must be sent to the Clerk of the Trust's office by 15th of January. A meeting of patrons then studied the applications and made a decision.

School Frocks made to the designs as required for Hutchesons' Grammar School in "Tobralco" material.

SENIOR GIRLS' style
School Frock and Knickers in "Tobralco"
Colours: Blue, Green, Beige, Helio, Pink. Sizes 32 to 48 ins.
12/9
rising 9d. per size.

JUNIOR GIRLS' style
School Frock and Knickers in "Tobralco"
Colours: Blue, Green, Beige, Helio, Pink. Sizes 24 to 38 ins.
9/9
rising 9d. per size.

PETTIGREW & STEPHENS LTD
Sauchiehall Street · Glasgow

Hutchesons' Grammar School, 1938.

John Taylor Williamson, 12 years of age.

John Williamson, 49 years, 84 Oswald St. He has been a tailor for 22 years, employing 2 or 3 workers. Income small. Oldest son was a Foundationer. One daughter at Hutchesons' Girls' School. One son earns 10/- per week. Three children in all, aged 15, 13 and 12. Teacher's report 'excellent'.

Rev James Black.
Note recorded that he was the brother of girls' cases Nos 29 and 30. Decision - admit. 1886

William Barr Wotherspoon, 8 years of age.

Mrs Elizabeth Wotherspoon (grandmother), 62 years of age. 301 Cathcart Rd. Boy's father was a wholesale stationer at Main St, Anderston for 3 years employing 4 workers. Boy's father and mother both dead. Grandmother was in business over 30 years in Main St., Anderston. Keeps boarders. No fixed income. Teacher's report - good.

Rev John Muir.
Decision - decline to admit. 1886

Originally the boys had to begin at seven years and be no more than eight years old on 1st of March in the year of admission. The names Hutcheson, Herbertson, Blair and Baxter, Barr, Wingate, Cunningham and Cameron were given preference.

Applicants to these charities must have attended an English School (a school which taught English) for six months before admission and have a certificate from a doctor that they were not suffering from any infectious disease. The boys had to attend the church service at St George's Tron Church every Sunday.

Each boy received a complete suit of clothes every April and October, a shirt, a pair of stockings and shoes and £3, half of which was paid at Martinmas in November and the rest at Whit-sunday in June, instead of board. When the boys left school they were presented with a Bible and up until 1787, on their being apprenticed, they had their indenture or fee paid by the Trust.

Hutchesons' Girls' School

Although proposals for the education of girls were made in 1842 it was 1876 before this became a reality. The girls were to be instructed in domestic topics by female teachers but in 'intellectual' ones by male teachers. The purposes given for educating girls were firstly to prepare them for domestic duties and secondly to increase their social value. The highest goal was to make them competent to serve in the Post Office and Telegraph Service.

In 1877 many girls obtained bursaries and attended the classes of the Association for the Higher Education of Women although there were no women permitted to graduate from Scottish universities until after 1892.

The Merchant Company of Edinburgh

In 1694 an Orphans and Trades Maidens Hospital for girls was opened in Edinburgh with funds given by Mrs Mary Erskine. Fifty girls were taught sewing, laundry work and the three Rs and were given £10 and a Bible on leaving. In 1871, one hundred girls from seven to seventeen years of age attended and the school was praised for introducing music which was played as the girls moved from one class to another every hour. A committee of ladies supervised the school and many of the girls boarded with local families.

In the same year George Watson, an Edinburgh merchant, left £12,000 to endow a school for the instruction of male children and grandchildren of members of the Edinburgh Merchant Company. Watson's Merchant Academy was opened in 1740, followed in 1814 by Daniel Stewart's for 'the children of industrious parents, whose circumstances did not enable them suitably to support and educate their children at other schools.' The pupils attended from seven to fourteen years and studied English, Latin, Greek, German, French, drill, fencing and gymnastics. James Gillespie's school, built in 1801, provided places for 150 boys.

Edinburgh Ladies College and, in 1841, George Watson's Ladies College , formerly the Merchant Maidens School and often referred to as Mary Erskine's School, were established for girls. All of these schools were open to the sons and daughters of burgesses whose fathers had fallen on hard times or who had died. The Merchant Company were the trustees and under the Endowment Act of 1869 applied for and received permission to convert them to day schools. These schools charged moderate fees. They also had a number of bursaries available and foundationers who came top on examination would be offered a place at one of the schools. On leaving, former pupils were given £7 for clothing.

George Heriot

In 1880 there were sixteen free Heriot Schools in Edinburgh teaching 4,400 pupils and in addition nine free evening schools offering the three Rs, grammar, French, German and drawing to 1,400 pupils over fourteen years of age. Surplus funds were used to provide five infant schools.

Dollar Academy

John Macnab was a herd laddie who attended the parish school until he had the inclination to see the world and set off for Leith. He sailed to London and through time made his fortune through investments in shipping and the slave trade. On his death he left in trust a large sum of money which in 1880 enabled the Trustees to build a large school which was to offer, as well as a basic education to the poor of the parish, a higher education:

> *In order that the more industrious and talented poor scholars might be able to obtain knowledge, which might fit them for rising above their present level in society, and for acquiring both riches and reputation in the world.*
>
> New Statistical Account, Parish of Dollar, 1841

It was decided to open the school to other children whose parents could afford fees and the masters were allowed to offer board and lodgings to them. It is reported that many pupils became gentlemen's gardeners after being apprenticed to the chief gardener of the school on completion of their education.

Robert Gordon's

Robert Gordon of Aberdeen was considered a miser. He was a merchant in Danzig who on his death in 1730 bequeathed all the money which he had saved to set up a 'hospital' - a school for the higher education of sons and grandsons of poor townsfolk of seven years of age upwards. From eleven to fifteen years of age they were to be taught book-keeping, geography and Latin and apprenticed to a trade. In 1800 there were eleven masters and 200 boys.

Boarding schools

Rural children were often boarders at the nearest secondary school. The Nicholson Institute, Stornoway, had pupils who walked home over ten miles on a Friday night, returning on a Sunday ready to attend school on the Monday. In 1834 an Education Enquiry was informed that 'poverty prevents small tenants, cottars, fishers and day-labourers from sending their children to board in the vicinity of the parochial school.' In 1908 travel and board and lodging was paid for them to live in dormitories during the week.

Loretto School

Loretto School, Musselburgh, was an intermediate school originally founded by Thomas Langhorne in the Episcopalian Parsonage. The large drawing room held twelve beds, a smaller room four beds. Lord Johnston, one of the earliest pupils, recalls that they were permitted to play golf on the links and marched in a crocodile to church, 'like a girls' school would.' Under its most influential headmaster, Hely Hutchinson Almond, by 1866 it was based on the English Public School system as was the Fettes College established in 1836.

> *The senior pupils who were reading for Oxford were called 'pewters' probably because they were allowed to drink their beer out of pewter tankards. There was a visiting drawing master, a dancing master, who was French, came on a Saturday morning. We used the Mound as an open air classroom. The gym was an old stable and cowshed with tarred boards and a felt roof. Sea bathing was compulsory every day and there was coal dust in the water. We had paper chases and were taken along the coast in a brake then had to run back. There were cross-country races known as Grinds. The Big Grind was from Selkirk to Peebles and the Little Grind was up the Pentlands.*
>
> Adapted from Charles Walker, who was a pupil in 1864, in *Loretto's Hundred Years, 1827 - 1927*, 1928

In 1864 the boys wore a Glengarry and in 1865 the Eton collar and short coat were introduced. This wasn't popular in Scotland and caused one mother to complain that they had 'made such a fright of my son.' Senior pupils were taken by brake to Gullane in the Autumn term to play golf and the barefooted children of Prestonpans gave chase and called after them 'poor oot, poor oot,' which was a request for a scramble of pennies.

Keil School

Keil School was set up in 1915 from the bequest of Sir William MacKinnon and his nephew Duncan Maxwell. It gave scholarships and was designed for boys from the Western Isles. It moved to Helenslee, Dumbarton the former home of Peter Denny, the shipbuilder, in 1925 when there were one hundred boys from thirteen to eighteen not just from Scotland but also from England and abroad. Queen Victoria School, Dunblane was opened after the Boer War to cater for the sons of army and navy personnel killed or wounded during the War. There were also boarding schools for girls. St Leonard's, in St Andrews, was opened in 1890 and St Columba's, Kilmalcolm. Many upper class and middle class girls were still taught at home by governesses.

The irony is that many of these endowed schools have gone on to become the most exclusive fee-paying schools whose ethos is far removed from the intentions of their founders.

Technical schools

In 1855 St Lawrence's School, Greenock, was opened by Monseigneur Eyre, Archbishop of Glasgow, to teach navigation, engineering and to provide a scientific training for seafarers. Many parochial schools had included navigation in the curriculum and in some towns science was promoted. In Falkirk, in 1878, there was a School of Science and Art and a technical school was established at Perth.

Allan Glen's Institution, Glasgow, was built in 1853 to educate and clothe 140 boys, sons of tradesmen. In 1875 it applied for a change of status and although retaining many bursaries it targeted the sons of the middle classes who wished to specialise in science and technical education. At the time it provided the latest laboratories and workshops.

Pupil teachers

From 1846 pupils who were talented might be able to receive a higher education by becoming pupil teachers. They supervised younger children and helped them to learn to read and write. They could do this from thirteen to eighteen years of age and were paid a small sum of money annually. James Maxton, who later became an M.P., won a Renfrew County Bursary to Hutchesons' Grammar School for three years. When he was fifteen years old he won a Hutcheson Trust which enabled him to be a pupil teacher for two years at Martyr's School, Glasgow at a salary of £15 per year. In 1902 he was admitted to the Glasgow Teachers Training College and to Glasgow University. This method of entering teaching continued up until 1906.

Education (Scotland) Act 1872

The Argyll Commission's enquiry into education from 1864-1867 found that there were 500,000 children of school age. 200,000 were reasonably literate but 90,000 did not attend school at all. Only 50% of city children attended school. This led to a committee under Lord Young forming a plan to reform education. The Education (Scotland) Act of 1872 was a most significant piece of legislation because it covered both primary and secondary schooling and enabled more children to achieve a secondary education:

It shall be the duty of every parent to provide elementary education in reading, writing and arithmetic for his children, between five and thirteen years of age.

School Boards

Elected School Boards, on which women who were ratepayers could serve, were to be set up in every parish and burgh in Scotland. Elections would take place every three years and the Boards were accountable to the ratepayers. Each Board must supply adequate accommodation, appoint teachers and oversee the curriculum. If not enough money was generated by fees then a levy was placed on the rates for the upkeep of schools. It was also the responsibility of the School Board after 1903 to ensure that children living in remote areas were educated. In order to comply with this, in such places, a teacher lived for five months of the year in the homes of each of his pupils in turn.

Parents were prosecuted and fined if they did not ensure that their children attended school. Elementary schooling was free and compulsory but there were exemptions. If a pupil was ten years of age and held an Inspector's Certificate of Proficiency in the three Rs they were not required to attend and half-timers were allowed under the Factory and Workshop Acts and the Mines Regulations Act. As can be seen from this sample table there were still many children who did not attend regularly:

Sample of number of pupils in attendance at Board Schools 1884		
Town	Possible	Actual
Pittenweem East	326	229
" West	219	153
Roxburgh	123	73
Fairnington	83	26
Heiton	78	60
Tarbolton	324	213
Annbank	469	400
Balmerino	129	71
Carluke Roman Catholic	132	103
Auchentibber " "	527	274
Isle of Harris	952	470

In 1884 there were 3,131 Board schools with 655,672 pupils, the average attendance being 448,242. In 1874 there were 4,407 pupils examined in higher subjects and in 1884 the number was 61,429, a massive increase yet the number of certificated teachers only doubled. In 1883 half-time education was allowed for children from ten to fourteen years of age but in 1901 all pupils had to remain at school until their fourteenth birthday.

From 1899 vocational courses leading to a merit certificate were taught in advanced divisions, a term which still existed unofficially in 1944. These pupils remained in their original school and did not go away to a secondary or higher grade school. In some areas elementary and higher grade did still physically occupy the same site. In 1908 an Intermediate Certificate (two years advanced division) was created. A Day School Certificate (lower and higher) was introduced which was taken two years before the Group Higher Leaving Certificate was attempted.

Scotch Education Department

This department was set up to administer the schools on a national basis. A Board of Education for Scotland was appointed. It was opposed by the presbyteries on religious grounds and Glasgow objected because it would encourage too many children to attend school and cost the ratepayers money.

The Education (Scotland) Act 1918 abolished School Boards and placed education directly under local government Education Authorities and changed the name of the department to the Scottish Education Department. This Act also gave public financial support to voluntary schools. In addition, schools previously maintained by the Roman Catholic Church were brought into the public sector through a guarantee in the 1918 Act that their denominational status would be continued. This latter move led to complaints of 'Rome on the rates.'

The raising of the school age to fifteen was first suggested in 1929 but the recession prevented it taking place. Again in 1936 it was overtaken by the threat of World War Two. At this time, however, science laboratories and technical rooms were being built for boys and upgraded cookery, laundry and needlework rooms for girls.

School life

Attendance

The log books of many schools report having to close because of bad weather. In the Highlands, in the 1840s, a gille an adharc - the boy of the horn - was a poor boy who for a fee of a penny a quarter from each scholar went round blowing on a horn as a sign that it was time to gather for the journey to school. He then, barefoot, set off through the snow. The wealthier boys wore boots to protect their feet from the cold.

Discipline

Although the cane was not the favourite means of corporal punishment in Scottish schools it was used occasionally, not only in the English type of public boarding school but also in the parochial schools. At Maryhill in 1873 quarrelsome boys or truants were sent to cut willow wands with which they were 'birched'. The name suggests that birch wood was the usual material for the cane.

The traditional means of corporal punishment in Scottish schools was the strap or belt also known as the tawse or the Lochgelly - from the town in which they were made. This was a thin piece of treated leather one or two inches wide which tailed into thongs. Unfortunately, it was not used only for misbehaviour but also if multiplication tables were not recited properly, if the answer to a sum was wrong, or a word misspelled or for any other failure to give a correct response. It was used often to quell talking in class.

Frederick Niven, the Scottish novelist who came back to Scotland as a boy from having lived in Latin America, was appalled by the harshness of the punishment he received at Hutchesons' Grammar School:

These thrashings with a leathern strap, supposedly on the palm of the hand but often on the wrist as well, causing pain that was slow to go, and sometimes leaving, for hours, a swelling as large as an egg on the blue-veined wrist.

Mrs Barry, Frederick Niven, 1933

Pupils would blow on their hands, spit on them or sit on them to help to relieve the pain. Some believed that placing a hair across their hand lessened the pain.

While he [the master] taught one group the others were left to work away on their own, and here the tawse played a very important part. If any of us were seen to be idling or trying to whisper to those near us, the Maister would fling the tawse to the culprit, who had to bring the instrument of torture to him to receive punishment.

Reminiscences of Colvend [1860s], Samuel Murdoch, in *The Gallovidian Annual*, 1929

A ruler or a long wooden pointer, which was used to indicate items on the map or blackboard, was also used to rap knuckles of those who talked out of turn. At Maryhill, in 1816, Charles Irvine the schoolmaster treated troublesome boys by making them stand on a stool wearing an old yellow wig. If they were really obstinate he put them down into the black hole, a cellar where he stored his potatoes, which was four feet deep and closed over by a hatch. They were left there to cool their heels.

*There is a happy land
By the old school,
Where Miss MacDonald stands,
Preaching like a fool.
Long legs and skinny jaws
She can fairly use the tawse
On the wee bit bairnies' paws
Three times a day.*

Traditional, Kirkcaldy

Methods and equipment

Up until 1944 slates and slate pencils were still used in schools. Pupils carried wee tins which contained a wet rag to clean the slate. Some classrooms had blackboards round the walls on which pupils could write with chalk. A teacher would walk behind the pupils to check their answers. Blackboards were usually of the easel and board type. Large cloth maps of the World were popular and showed all the bright red areas which belonged to the British Empire.

The teacher sat at a high desk so that he or she could watch over the heads of the class. Apart from the infant room the leather Lochgelly strap was always visible. Desks often were double with an iron base to which were attached two wooden slats which could be raised and lowered and on which pupils had to sit all day long. They were arranged in rows with passages in between. In the upper school china inkwells were set into the desks and it was the job of the monitor to fill them up. Boys would soak blotting paper with ink and then, using their rulers as a catapult, let the pellet fly across the room. In mixed schools they would dip the pigtails of the girls in the ink.

Pens were slim pieces of wood with metal nibs which could be re-placed. They were easily damaged and if the nib was bent the writing would be poor. Writing was considered important and the script in many jotters was beautifully formed. Lined green books with pre-written sentences were given out and these had to be copied using thick and thin lines. Left handed pupils were at a disadvantage as they often literally blotted their copy book. Blotting paper was used to dry the ink.

Curriculum

In Board schools the three Rs were still the main subjects taught. Mental arithmetic was the terror of many pupils. Everyone stood and when the pupil knew the answer they sat down. One pupil would then be asked to say it out loud. If a pupil did not want to be considered a dunce they sometimes took a gamble and sat down, even if they did not know the correct answer, crossing their fingers that they would not be the one to be asked. Multiplication tables were

learned by heart and examined every day. Reading was learned from letter cards followed by a different book for each standard and a number of spelling words had to be learned every day. Scottish history and geography was taught and pupils also learned about other parts of the world. Religion, Protestant based, was seen as important in Board schools and the Lord's Prayer was recited every morning. The Shorter Catechism was taught and examined every day and Bible stories were read aloud to the class. Singing, drawing and reciting poetry were permitted and the study of citizenship - local government and learning about the local community - was encouraged.

Physical education

After 1872 many new schools were built by the School Boards. There were separate playgrounds, entrance doors and cloakrooms for boys and girls. When the bell rang the pupils would line up and march in to music. Upstairs school classrooms were often arranged around a gallery. This looked down into the main hall which might double as the drill hall. Drill was the usual name for physical education rather than gymnastics or P.E. This was introduced in 1895 and was often taught by ex-soldiers recruited for the task. In some schools it was part of the duties of the 'janny', as the school janitor or caretaker was affectionately called. Many parents were unhappy at the fact that their sons had to remove their jackets and jerseys to take part and a greater number were offended if their daughters, whose drill lesson was taken by their class teacher, were expected to perform exercises dressed in their blue or grey flannel knickers.

In 1900, at the time of recruiting men for the Boer War, it was discover-ed that their physical condition was often poor. Aberdeen Trades Council, in 1905, proposed that power should be given to all local authorities to provide meals for schoolchildren and to make provision for their physical efficiency and that this matter should be addressed by Parliament.

Accordingly the School Boards were instructed to provide a higher

standard of physical education and when new schools were built gymnasiums were designed with wall bars for reverse-hanging and other climbing exercises, and equipment might include leather 'horses' or bucks with two wooden handles or a tumbling box which could be raised or lowered in height for exercises, and specially designed beams which were lowered from the ceiling for balancing and swinging. Ropes for climbing also hung from the ceiling and two ropes were used together to perform 'flying angels' - an exercise where both hands were released from the rope and the pupil was supported by the feet which were wound around the ropes. Wooden benches for balancing, bean bags and hoops completed the picture.

In the 1920s playing fields were obtained so that pupils should have more exercise and football, swimming, hockey and netball became popular.

Toilets

At first toilets were often primitive, being dry-closets, but even modern flush toilets in the new schools were built out in the playground. A wall made a roofless passage - on one side there were toilets with doors, although often these were simply holes in the ground lined with china. There was a high cistern with a chain. They froze up in winter, were never very efficient, usually smelt, but existed up until 1944 and after.

Fees

At one time fees for higher education were levied for each subject and only the well-off could afford to study a wide variety. In 1873 fees in primary classes 1-3 were 10d per month, in classes 4-5 they were 1/- and in class 6 pupils paid 1/3d. Many secondary schools charged fees up until 1944 when an Education Act finally abolished them. In addition, all school books and jotters had to be paid for, so if there were several children of school age in a family education was costly. This often led to boys being given their chance at the expense of their sisters. In some schools teachers collected and kept the fees as part of their salary. School Boards were wary of charging education to the rates.

Fun!

There were two or three annual gala days in our school life at Barnbarroch. There was the Candlemas 'bleezes' each 2nd of February... On that day we went to school dressed in our Sunday best with a shilling in our pockets for the Maister. In return each scholar was given an orange and a dram of hot whisky toddy... The Maister would entertain us with a song or story and...Robert McKinnell, a farmer, came regularly with his bagpipes to play some of those stirring old Scottish melodies...Another day to be remembered was the breaking up for our summer vacation. There was no school board to fix the date and the scholars took it upon themselves to remind the Maister that the holidays were due. This they did by fixing on the handle of the door a wisp of ripe corn as a hint that the harvest was about to be begun when the service of some of the children would be needed...The Christmas and New Year vacation was limited to a day or two at the most. As Christmas approached one or two of the older scholars gathered sufficient from the others to purchase a goose, which they bought from a neighbouring farm and carried to the school alive and gaily decked in ribbons... The Maister usually dismissed the scholars for the rest of the day.

Reminiscences of Colvend [1860s],
Samuel Murdoch <u>in</u> *The Gallovidian Annual*, 1929.

Truancy

Parents could be summoned before the School Board for their children's non-attendance and fined up to 15/- or ten days in jail. Often girls were kept at home to look after younger children. One girl in Stirling saw all her younger brothers and sisters sent

Glasgow Trades and Labour Council

DEMAND
Free Books for all School Children

THE decision of the Glasgow Education Authority to withdraw Free Books for School Children will mean that the children will be informed by their teachers that their parents must provide them with Books.

Parents are advised not to provide Books for the following reasons :

(1) Education is a communal necessity and responsibility. EVERY CHILD should be given free and full opportunity to become equipped for life. It is proposed that only necessitous children will receive Free Books ; this means an inquisition by Officials and a Committee similar in operation to a Charity Organisation Society.

(2) The decision is calculated by a majority of the Authority to gain the favour of those electors who look on a reduction of rates as a sign of sound administration.   NOTE—The election of the Education Authority takes place in the Spring of 1922.

(3) The figures given by the Education Authority as to the cost of Books indicate the hardship that will be imposed on Working Class parents. Calculated on 189,000 scholars, the average cost for Books per scholar will be :—

	Per Scholar.
All Schools including Higher Grade -	7/5½
Elementary Schools - - - -	5/10½
Elementary Schools less 2nd Readers -	5/-
Higher Grade Schools - - - -	30/-

What will this mean to a parent having 3 children at school?

1 Child attending Higher Grade School -	30/-
2 Children attending Elementary School -	11/9
Total -	**41/9**

The Authority claim that 3d. per £ is the saving on rates by withdrawing Free Books. It has been ascertained that the assessable valuation in the Glasgow Parish of a house rented at £18 equals £10 16/-, which at 3d. per £ equals 2/8½. That a house rented at £28 equals £16 16/-, which at 3d. per £ equals 4/2½.

Taking the above figures, to purchase books will mean to the parents 41/9. If rated on an £18 rental or £28 rental, the cost will be 2/8½ and 4/2½ respectively.

(4) 172 out of 194 Headmasters have reported to the Education Authority that the provision of Free Books is of enormous advantage in the actual class work.

Refuse to purchase Books for the foregoing reasons and compel the Education Authority to continue the supply of Free Books to all School Children.

CIVIC PRESS, LTD., Printers.

STUC Library.

singling turnips in the fields, grouse beating and herding. In Perthshire there were three main harvests - fruit, grain and potato - and few pupils would be found at their desks during these times.

...There was a big batch of the older scholars away. The clerk read a letter from the headmaster, in which it was stated that the idea had got abroad that child labour was to be permitted for the potato gathering. He had already been approached by one farmer on the subject. Mr Bonthron thought that during these exceptional times, when so much poverty was about they should relax their rules...

East Fife Record, 4th October, 1915

to school in turn but she, the eldest, was never given the chance. Sometimes children found work before their fourteenth birthday and decided not to attend school. This was frowned upon by the authorities. In 1900 at Twechar a girl who was in service at the age of thirteen and had been taken 'down the coast' by her mistress was ordered to return to school. Also in 1900, Alexander Miller, aged thirteen, who worked as an iron dresser at the Lion Foundry in Kirkintilloch was sent back to school. His father protested because he would lose the boy's wages.

Daughters were often kept at home for up to three days every week to help their mothers. Boys and girls were kept off school for the 'tattie howkin' - potato lifting,

Parents incapable of ensuring that their children would attend school could be asked by the School Board to permit them to be sent to an industrial school and unless they agreed could be prosecuted. One parent in Campeltown in 1900, gave the excuse that his son could never be found when it was time for school and the Sheriff advised him to tie his son to the bedrail.

School Boards saw non-attendance as loss making as the fees were not paid. This could result in a loss of 1d per day. Attendance Officers were appointed to investigate the absence of pupils and reported to the School Boards who then interviewed the parents. They could be prosecuted by the Justices of the Peace or the Magistrates Court.

Work

Children were valuable. From the age of five they could earn a wage which added to the family income. Orphans were also attractive to employers as they could be used as cheap labour in factories or mills. Up to 75% of workers in industry could be children.

Children as young as five years of age may begin to be useful, and are even employed in different branches of woollen manufacture which are singularly adapted to their infant state.

Essays in Trade, Commerce, Manufactures and Fisheries of Scotland, David Loch, 1778

In both rural and urban life and in their own homes children had work to do as soon as they could toddle. Children as young as five were used, often on Sundays when the factory or mill closed down, to clean the machinery. Children worked as scavengers as they were small and could crawl underneath the machinery to remove the waste material. This was a dirty and dusty job which clogged their noses and they were filthy from spilled oil.

A factory inspector found that in 1819 orphans were being sent two or three hundred miles from their birthplace to work. Groups of them were offered at auction and went to the highest bidder. In 1836 an owner made an agreement with a Parish Council to take one mentally handicapped child with every twenty 'sound' children to relieve them of a drain on the poor rate.

Cities had a particularly poor record when it came to caring for orphans. Once they found them employment they ignored them. Working in textile mills for seventeen hours a day was common. Often they

Children working in brickworks.

had to stand at all times, or worked in cramped positions. Many children lived in the mill, in rooms with iron grills which covered the windows, or in nearby bothies. They were not even permitted to attend church on Sundays in case they would try to run away. They had no-one to turn to and were beaten by guards at the least excuse.

In 1838, a girl from the Town's Hospital of Glasgow was sent to work in Kirkintilloch and was bound to serve and obey the manufacturer for five years. If she should be ill and unable to work then for every lost day she must add two days without pay to the end of her contract. A two year old child was found working in a lace manufacturers and children of three carried bricks at a brickwork.

Overseers were occasionally fined or dismissed for excessively punishing a child but the masters paid the fine and the overseer would find work in a neighbouring mill. John Hendry, Kirkintilloch, was imprisoned for assaulting three apprentices in 1845:

Having the habit of flogging them most unmercifully, hanging them up by their wrists, and then inflicting cruel chastisement on their naked bodies, and with plunging them in a state of nudity into a well.

History of the Working Classes, Thomas Johnston, 1932

Children's Employment Commission

In 1842 a Children's Employment Commission was set up. They discovered that a girl, in 1840, too sick to work, had been sent to jail for thirty days under the Masters and Servants Act 1800, and a girl of thirteen years, in 1842, was transported to the Colonies for a minor offence. In 1843 the Commission was successful in having a law passed to prevent very young children being employed in the factories, mines and mills.

Collieries

Colliers in East Fife were expected to provide a bearer to bring out the coal and daughters as young as eleven years were found down the pit, up to their calves in water carrying one cwt. of coal. At Edmonstone Pit, Midlothian, a girl of ten worked twelve to fourteen hours per day carrying coals. Her father earned, in total, 6/- per week. He told the Commission of Enquiry into the Employment of Children in 1842 that 'it's ower sair for females'. At Loanhead, a girl of eight worked from 2am - 1pm carrying one and a half cwts. of coal on her back along the pit road and she was beaten if she disobeyed an order. Another girl of eleven, worked from 5am - 5pm weekdays and all night on Friday until noon on Saturday.

Older children, even girls, worked as drawers or hurriers.

On short shifts, I work from eight in the morning till six at night; on long ones until ten at night. Occasionally we work all night. At the wall face where the miner cuts the coal, I fill a bogie with two and a half or three

Coal trappers, 19th century.

hundredweights of coal. I then hook it on to my chain and drag it through the seam which is 26 - 28 inches high till I get it to the main road - a good distance, 200 - 300 yards. There I fill it into a cart. The pavement I drag it over is wet, and I have at all times to crawl on hands and feet. It is sad, sweating and sore fatiguing work.

Evidence to the *Commission of Enquiry into the Employment of Children*, Margaret Hipps, 1842

Small boys of four or five worked as trappers in the pits. They opened the air-door to let the wagons of coal through. They had a candle for light. At Tranent a boy of ten was found sitting in water for up to thirteen hours per day. If he fell asleep he was beaten.

Sometimes there were accidents with run-a-way trucks and boys were crushed by the weight of the trucks. David Neill, six, an orphan, was fed on bread. He and some others tried to run away but they were caught and flogged. Under the bond of indenture these children were slaves.

In Lanarkshire, Alexander Macdonald, who later became a

teacher and agitator for workers' rights, worked down the pit at eight years of age and only saw daylight on a Sunday for three months of the year.

Lord Astley, later the Earl of Shaftesbury, presented a Mines Regulations Bill to Parliament in 1871 limiting the hours of women and children to twelve per day and no child was to work in a mine under thirteen years of age. The coal masters fought this and it was changed so that children between ten and thirteen were only allowed to work three days per week and no females were permitted to work underground. The amended Bill was enacted in 1872 when a Mines Act prohibited children under fifteen from working in mines.

Textiles

New Lanark

Robert Owen, praised for his enlightened stance towards children, found on coming to New Lanark, in 1799, that the five hundred children who were employed there had no holidays and worked thirteen hours per day for a six day week. He prevented children working in the mills until they reached their tenth birthday and he also campaigned for others to follow his lead.

We only work ten and a half hours a day now, and we have meal breaks for breakfast and dinner. I work in the mill as a

piecer, joining the broken threads. The mill's no' a bad place to work. Och, you have to take care. The machines dinnae stop for no-one, so there's aye wee accidents, and sometimes worse.

Annie McLeod, aged 10 in 1820 in *The Annie McLeod Experience*, New Lanark Conservation Trust

Lennoxmill

I had several jobs in the works before I commenced my apprenticeship of seven years to print-cutting. One of these jobs was working at the 'warm end' of the blotching-house; there we had to stand over nearly red-hot plates, and keep stretching out the cloth as it kept passing over the drying rollers.

Another boy and I took it in turns, fifteen minutes at a time. I have seen when I came out to cool that I could hardly touch the metal buttons on my clothes, they were so hot...Another job I had gave me an opposite experience. It was working at the Lade, streaming cloth in the water. This was pleasant in the summer months, but not in the winter. All the same we had often to stand over the boards and the cold water from 6am till 12pm on many occasions.

I will ever remember one very cold night, when the thermo-meter fell nearly to zero, that my comrades and I were all frozen to the boards, cloth and all. Our leggings were covered with ice, and fingers benumbed with cold. My comrades and I latterly were crying and had to be lifted from the boards to which we were frozen... This exposure to cold I had to endure for sixteen hours on a stretch for the magnificent pay of 6d per day and 1d per hour for overtime.

John Young's Reminiscences, 1841 in *The Parish of Campsie*, John Cameron, 1892

In 1859, eleven to eighteen hours daily were being worked by children in the bleachfields of the west of

Scotland. They worked over stoves heated to 80-100 degrees. The skin of their hands and feet was blistered. Even the youngest children were forced to work two or three nights per week when the industry was at its height. If they fell asleep they were beaten. A Bleachfields Bill was presented to Parliament in 1860 to curb the excessive hours worked.

Tear-boys

Every block printer had a tearer working with him. These children carried out dangerous and dirty work, often beneath the machines. They worked from 5.15am till 6pm for 2/6d per week. As revealed in the 1891 census for Garscube Road, Glasgow, the majority of children working were in the textile mills.

Every day at twelve noon the biggest tear-boy at Dawsholm Print Works, Glasgow, was sent to the factory store (truck shop) for whisky in a clay piggin. Sugar was added to this and all the men drank their bucketful. This may be the origin of the slang expression that someone who drinks a lot, 'enjoys a good bucket'.

Drawers and spoolers

Boys and girls were employed as drawers. Their job was to stand in the simple fit - a hole at the side of the loom - to pull down the threads of the shuttle as instructed. These threads were of different colours and kept the pattern correct. They worked barefoot under the loom which was oosey and oily and in very cramped conditions. Spoolers were boys who put the spools of thread onto the loom and turned them as required.

The weaver said unto his son
The day that he was born,
"God's blessing on your curly pow,
You'll gang tae the pirns in the morn."

Traditional

The pirn was the name for the bobbin which carried the thread.

Juvenile strikes

At the Anchor Mill of J. and P. Coats in Paisley in 1904 the girls came out on strike. They gathered at Seedhill. The boy spoolers came out in support and led by a piper marched with them through the town. Some of the girls rode in carts and tormented the police by throwing pease meal at them. In 1907, when the spoolers went on strike, the girls in turn supported them and some girls were arrested for attacking the police with twelve inch hatpins.

Child workers, Neilston Mill strike meeting, 1910.

Nobs

Nob was the name given to young boys and girls who were brought into the print works to break strikes.

Sweated labour

In the 1840s there were children working in the manufacture of garments. Many worked at home sewing on buttons for a pittance. Others worked in uncomfortable conditions with poor light and ventilation. Peter Henrietta, a tailor in Glasgow, made a study of these conditions. He reported that in one room, 7ft x 9ft, there were three women and five children. Two of the children had their heads shaved from diptheria. Only when middle-class families began to realise that clothing for their children could be coming from infection ridden and verminous dens did they begin to support action against these sweatshops. In the 1880s conditions were still poor.

The first job I got was the finishin' of dongaree jackets, sewin' buttons on them, and things like that. I was up in the mornin' at six and went to bed the next mornin' at one, and hard at it all the time. I wasn't sleepin'. Sunday was the same as any other day; always the needle.

The Rat Pit, Patrick MacGill, 1915

All day long they worked together in the murky cavern sorting the rags. The smell of the place was awful, suffocating almost; the damp and mouldy rags gave forth an unhealthy odour; dust rose from those that were drier and filled the place and the throats of the workers.

The Rat Pit, Patrick MacGill, 1915

Chimney climbing boys

Boys were beaten to force them to climb up chimneys to sweep away the soot. They had salt rubbed onto their skin to toughen it but they were often found to have skinned knees and elbows and were badly burned. Sometimes they became stuck in the bend of a chimney. In those circumstances a smaller child would be sent up to attach a rope to the first. The rope was then tugged until the boy was released. Many boys died as a result of burns or were suffocated by soot. Sometimes a chimney had to be demolished to rescue the body because it was blocking the air-flow. Boys would be carried from room to room to avoid

Chimney climbing boy.

dirtying the floors or carpets.

Even after the 1840 Act was passed banning climbing-boys, or girls, as late as the 1860s the practice was found to be increasing. In 1845 a nine year old in Glasgow was pushed up a chimney and his employer was fined £2.2.0 (two guineas) and the owner of the house was also fined 10/6d. The Employment Commissioners reported that magistrates were reluctant to fine the employers because they felt that the fine of £5 was excessive. An Act was passed in 1880 which finally brought an end to this torture.

Accidents

In the first six months of 1850 there were 183 accidents to children in Scottish factories reported to factory inspectors but they turned the blame on the carelessness of the children. In Aberdeen a boy lost his finger while working a saw. The owner was fined 30/- but the boy's father was fined £1 for his son's carelessness.

Message boys and girls

From the 1880s onwards shops began to expand and there was always an opening for message boys or girls. These home deliveries continued up until World War Two and after. Often a bicycle with a specially made basket attached to the front was used. Other boys and girls went with the milk cart which stopped at each house to fill enamel jugs or small churns with fresh milk. Those whose round included tenements had all the stairs to climb.

Those who were van-boys were envied. They were allowed to sit up on the seat beside the driver until they reached their destination. All sorts of goods were delivered to shops from bakeries and warehouses. During World War Two there was a shortage of labour and boys were allowed to leave school early to help out.

David Conchie was employed by Dumfries Co-operative Society, while he was still thirteen, as a van boy and loved looking after the horses which drew the carts and vans. To keep his feet warm straw was pushed into the toes of his boots.

The Scottish Council for Women's Trades carried out an inquiry in Edinburgh in 1901 into the employment of children as messengers. It was conducted through the headmasters of twenty four Edinburgh schools and covered 1,238 children who were working as message boys or girls. Dairies employed 35.8%, newsagents - 13.6%, grocers - 11.5%, bakers and confectioners - 10%. The other 3% worked for butchers, bootmakers, dressmakers, fruiterers, in theatres as call-boys or programme sellers. Some children worked for more than one trade.

For the extreme hours of work we must go to the grocers, bakers, butchers and shops of that kind. - four hours or so daily after school, and twelve, thirteen and fourteen hours on Saturdays are quite common. One boy of thirteen is stated to work from 7am on Saturday till midnight - 17 hours. As many as 282 of the children work for a period of twelve hours or more on Saturday.

The Employment of Children. Report of an Inquiry conducted for the Scottish Council for Women's Trades, 1901

Of those who worked over forty hours per week one boy was ten years of age. He worked for both a dairy and a grocer: 6am - 8am for the dairy, 4.30pm - 9pm for the grocer. He worked all day on a Saturday. He earned 1/6d per week from the dairy and 2/6d from the grocer. The headmaster's comment was that he was bright and healthy.

Another two boys, aged twelve and thirteen, worked as trace boys, leading horses by the rein. They worked 7-8.30am and 5-7pm when they had a break for tea. They worked again from 8.30pm - 11.30 or 11.45pm. On Saturdays they worked 7am - 11.30 or 11.45pm with an hour and a half for dinner. Their schoolwork was below standard. One of them was an orphan.

A girl of thirteen worked for an ice-cream shop, daily 4-9pm. She served in the shop and also looked after the baby, taking it for walks. She was well fed but not very intelligent.

Headmasters and teachers felt that long hours did affect the children, making them too tired to concentrate and leading them astray.

The teachers say they [the pupils] come in and sleep. The children at this school come from a good class, the argument therefore that work keeps them off the streets does not apply. Is the work light? Yes, on the whole; it is the protracted hours which make it severe. Does it train them for future work? No, rather it makes them pick up bad ways from the older shop boys, e.g. smoking; the children are put too soon with working boys.

The Employment of Children. Report of an Inquiry conducted for the Scottish Council for Women's Trades, 1901

Sometimes the children go to work of their own accord, sometimes their mother sends them. The mothers often deny that their children sell papers when they actually do. People with small shops are the worst for they employ their own children so long. It has the worst effect on education. Is the children's word reliable, or do they exaggerate? They generally try to give the hours when asked less than they actually are. A number of those returned did not give their names for fear.

The Employment of Children. Report of an Inquiry conducted for the Scottish Council for Women's Trades, 1901

Domestic service

Traditionally for girls at around twelve years of age, from less well-off backgrounds who did not work on a farm or in a factory, the choice was to become domestic servants. There was always a demand for assistant housemaids, kitchen maids and skivvies. Housemaids rose early, 6 o'clock in summer and 6.30am in winter. Before breakfast they swept and dusted the public rooms which were used by the family, including the drawing-room in case any guests should arrive. Fires were lit and coal carried. Hot water was taken up to the bedrooms in jugs to allow the members of the family to wash. Kitchen maids learned from the cook how to prepare a meal and skivvies scrubbed floors and washed up dishes and pots.

Wages were paid quarterly or half-yearly. Domestic servants received board and lodgings, one afternoon per week off and one day off per month. They ate in the kitchen and had half-an-hour for breakfast and supper and an hour for dinner which was usually in the middle of the day.

In 1900 girls going into service from institutions were sent out with 2 aprons, 2 yards of body lining and cloth for 1 dress, 4 yards of cotton, 2 chemises, 2 pair of drawers, 1 hat, 2 handkerchiefs, 1 jacket, 1 plain petti-coat, 1 serge petticoat, 2 scarves, 2 semmits, 2 pair of hose, 1 set of stays, print material for 2 dresses, buttons, 4 yards of braid, 1½ yards ribbon, 1 brush, 2 combs and a large box.

National Vigilance Association

This Association was set up in 1910 to oversee the welfare of girls coming to work in the cities from the Highlands and Ireland. The lady volunteers met them on their arrival at railway stations and at the docks and offered them temporary accommodation in a hostel. They also ran training centres for girls of fourteen and over who wished to become domestic servants.

The Salvation Army

The Salvation Army had training homes for protestant girls who required discipline and its Women's Help Committee provided them with domestic training.

United British Women's Protected Emigration Association

Lady Helen Munro-Ferguson has established a Training Home at

Raith, Kirkcaldy, where would-be colonists can obtain an excellent all-round training in domestic work, dressmaking etc. The terms are very moderate, and certificates are given after a year's residence. This training is specially useful for better class girls who wish to go out as 'lady-helps'.

The Association makes all arrangements for the passage, etc., sending out girls in parties under the charge of a matron, who looks after them during the voyage and on their arrival in the distant colony. There is also a loan fund to help needy deserving cases.

Seventeenth Report of the Glasgow Union of Women Workers, 1901

The Central Committee on Women's Training and Employment under the auspices of the Ministry of Labour ran grant-aided establishments which trained girls for domestic work. They had a residential home at Lenzie and day centres at Coatbridge, Greenock and Burntisland. They sent girls to work at selected farmhouses and manses in rural districts and some-times sent them overseas.

3,000 girls have been placed in situations in a healthy country environment. The majority come from over-crowded city homes suffering from long term unemployment.

Report, The Central Committee on Women's Training and Employment, 1901

Mary, who was sent by the Queen Margaret's Settlement in Glasgow to convalesce at the St Leonard's School Seniors Convalescent Home, St Andrews, in 1912 made such a good recovery that she was invited to stay on as a maid and became the Matron's only full-time help.

Street trading

Children worked on the streets as match-sellers, flower sellers, newspaper sellers, shoe-blacks and sold split sticks for firewood. They worked in all weather, often from 5am - 7pm, for 6d per day. In Clydebank, in 1909, it was reported

in the local paper that fifty boys and girls under sixteen years of age were acting as street traders within the Burgh but were not trading during school hours. The children worked from 6am - 8am and from 5pm - 10pm. They were mainly selling newspapers although a few worked on market stalls.

The work does not help boys learn good work habits; on the contrary, it is often difficult to make them learn good trades afterwards, being used to working about the streets.

The Employment of Children. Report of an Inquiry conducted for the Scottish Council for Women's Trades, 1901

In 1912, the Scottish Council for Women's Trades proposed a motion at the Scottish Trades Union Congress that:

recognising that the employment of boys and girls in street-trading has not only serious moral results for themselves, but is also a cause of great economic evils through the army of unskilled and casual workers which it produces, [Congress] resolves that, in the interests of the whole community, it is desirable to prohibit the employment of boys under seventeen, and girls under eighteen, in street trading.

The delegates heard from speakers that 75% of boys involved in street trading eventually went to prison and that 60% of those in industrial schools were also street traders. Money earned in this manner was spent on gambling and betting on cards and pitch and toss. An amended version was adopted.

Shipbuilding

I left school on my fourteenth birthday and started work in the office at a warehouse in the town. I then moved to the office at Fairfields Shipyard in the Autumn of 1915. The head of the Time Office asked for me to replace a boy going on to be an apprentice. All the men had brass tokens which they put into a time box in their department

David Conchie, van boy, 1939.

when they arrived for each shift. We collected these and brought them to be checked and replaced the tokens afterwards.

There was a great perk called the Boys' Box. The men would put money into a box at holidays and New Year. This was split amongst the time boys and was a welcome bonus. When I started my apprenticeship in 1917 I worked from 6am - 6pm every day except Saturday when I had a half day and only worked from 6am - noon. Breakfast was an hour and a half from 8am - 9.30am and dinner from 1pm - 2pm.

Interview with Robert Livingstone, 1996

There was no real choice of trade. In those days [1930s] you were lucky to get a job of any kind. I left school at fourteen and worked as a van boy with the Clydebank Laundry. And then when I was about fourteen and a half my father took me to the yard; to what they call the Platers' Market. And the foreman came and picked you out, asked for your particulars, that's how you got started. The

wage I started with was 15/8 a week. I worked as a marker boy for the Deck Squad until I was sixteen then I naturally started my time at the plating.

Making Ships and Men, Alan McKinlay, 1995

Factory and Workshop Acts

A Factory Education Bill was presented in 1843 but was not well received and the *Scotch Reformers' Gazette* reported that the ministers of Glasgow felt that this Bill was a curb on the freedom of the employers:

by prohibiting employment in factories of all children and young persons who are not able to present certificates of their having been instructed in schools under the Government inspection, thereby tyrannically depriving employers of the liberty to receive, and the workers to give, the service which may be most convenient and desirable for both.

Scottish Reformers' Gazette, 20th May, 1843

The Bill was withdrawn but in 1844 a Factory Act was passed restricting the hours of women and children to twelve per day. Holidays were to be agreed and machinery was to be made safer by attaching guards. There also had to be a minimum of half-time education up until thirteen years of age although exemptions could be made.

From 1878 to 1895 several Acts were passed to try to ensure a safer and healthier environment for child workers. A child under eleven could not be employed in any factory or workshop. At fourteen, or thirteen if they had passed school Standard 5, a birth certificate and medical certificate were needed before they could be employed in many factories and workshops.

Half-timers were permitted to work either morning or afternoon, or on alternate days for six hours and school attendance certificates had to be obtained by their employers. No children were to be employed during the night or on Sundays and proper provision for meal times and holidays had to be made. No children were to be employed above or below ground in a colliery under Acts of 1872 and 1887.

The Education (Scotland) Acts 1873 - 1893 stated that no children under ten could be in employment. No-one between ten and fourteen, unless holding a Labour Certificate or a Certificate of Merit, or who had passed Standard 3 and was a half-timer could be employed during school hours or after 7pm in winter or 9pm in summer.

The first Scottish Trades Union Congress, 1897, passed a resolution calling for the age of full-time employment for all children to be raised to fourteen years and half-timers to twelve years. This did not happen until the Employment of Children Act 1903 which stated that boys between ten and twelve could only work for one and a half hours before school and one and a half hours after school but they could work for six hours on Saturdays or during school holidays. A break of one and a half hours for a meal was necessary after three hours work. Boys from twelve to fourteen could work for two hours before and after school and for eight hours on Saturdays and holidays but must have a break of one hour after four hours.

Girls aged ten to fourteen could work two hours in the afternoon only and six hours Saturdays and holidays. In addition no child must lift, carry or move anything so heavy that injury could be caused nor be employed under dangerous conditions injurious to life, limb and health. If a medical practitioner signed a certificate for injury to a child caused by work it was used as evidence against an employer and led to a fine of up to £2, or for a further offence up to £5.

Farming

It was taken for granted that children in rural areas would help with the numerous chores around the croft, farm or holding. Girls from an early age churned butter, gathered thistles for down which was used in bedding, plucked hens, the feathers of which were used for pillows and the tail feathers for dusters or for cleaning pots and girdles. They also drove cattle, brought in pails of water from the well, milked the cows, fed hens and collected the eggs. If a lamb needed to be bottle fed it was often the girls of the family who were given the job. They looked after the younger children, stacked peats and gathered blaeberries, brambles and gooseberries to make jam or jelly.

Boys would eke out the family budget by catching cormorants, ducks and geese. They set traps for rabbits, guddled trout and caught salmon. They could earn seasonal money by hoeing turnips, walking sheep to market, grouse beating, collecting stones from the fields and taking them to be crushed for bottoming for roads. Foresters needed a hand with clearing dead wood and the remains could be chopped up for firewood. At night they had to help in the making of rag rugs for the home along with the rest of the family.

After twelve years of age boys might be employed at the shooting lodges to look after the horses and draw the stag carcasses from the hill on a wattle sledge. Being allowed to learn to plough was the ambition of many boys and when mechanisation came in learning to drive a tractor was the aim.

Fishing

Before and after school children in fishing communities would be busy splitting open mussels for bait. In Galloway, at Palnackie, there is still an annual flounder tramping championship and in the 1920s boys and girls joined in the fun. Elsewhere it was razor fish, or muskins as they were called, which were tempted to the surface by the fisher walking backwards, barefooted; then as soon as a movement was noted a curved handled walking stick was thrust beneath the sand and a spear with a triangular barb was inserted beneath the fish which was hooked and placed in a creel. The only danger was that if they forgot to keep a lookout and were standing on a sandbank they could be cut off by the fast flowing tide.

Boys would also swim across a river mouth with a trawl net attached to their head to earn a few pennies. Near Wick boys used to be paid to kill the rats which harried the henhouse of the fishcurer. A galley boy was employed on a fishing boat as an assistant cook, washer up and fish gutter. Hacks on his fingers would nip from the salt used to preserve the fish. He was allowed to drink whisky with the men and even to 'stand his hand' - pay for a round in the pub. Boys loved to be taken to sea as young as possible and they

Boys with catch, probably their pay, 1930s.

would learn to steer with the handle of a brush attached to the tiller.

Girls helped in the gutting and drying of fish. The gutting required nimble fingers and many hacks and cuts occurred. As the herring were preserved in salt this meant that their fingers nipped despite the bandages which they always wore. Cod-liver oil was also extracted from the fish and had to be bottled. It was not used only for medicinal purposes but also to soften leather in the boot factories and for burning in cruzies to give light.

Sometimes girls went with their mother or grandmother to carry the creels of fish to sell them at the nearest town. Boarded out children were taken in by fishing communities and they also had their share of the work to do. Learning to mend nets was a useful skill as was whipping a rope. Seaweed was a valuable commodity which was gathered above the tide line. It was used as a medicine, in the manufacture of cosmetics and as a fertiliser.

Crime Prevention and Punishment

Up before the Juvenile Delinquency Board, 1890s.

Many children were driven to a life of crime in order to eat while many more also had crimes committed against them. They were beaten and locked away in cupboards under stairs for all sorts of misdemeanours and this occurred, especially in Victorian times, in the houses of the rich as well as the poor. Children were supposed to be obedient and carry out the wishes of the head of the household. Schoolmasters acted *in loco parentis* and, while under their care, took over punishing the child for the slightest offence.

At the Sheriff Criminal Court...Andrew Brunton, carter, Leith, pleaded guilty to having cruelly treated his son, a boy seven years of age, on many occasions...the boy's mother died about twelve months ago, and since that time the prisoner had repeatedly beaten the boy on various parts of his naked body with leather straps, one of which had a buckle upon it, and the boy's body was in consequence of the usage much bruised and marked. The Sheriff sentenced the prisoner to 9 months imprisonment.

The North British Agriculturist, 25th September, 1867

Children had few rights and could be sold into slavery or work which was every bit as bad and then the employers could punish them and withhold their wages if they should fall asleep or not work fast enough to their way of thinking. This often meant that they had no money to buy food and were driven to steal.

Fagins

There were many willing 'Fagins' who taught children to be pickpockets. One of these was Hugh Thomson of Edinburgh who reset the proceeds of the crimes. The pupils usually graduated to further crimes such as housebreaking. In 1843 Preger, aged fourteen, and Shields, aged ten, were caught in Edinburgh after stealing a musical box which played the *Bluebells of Scotland*. They had been sent by their minder to steal it from a house. It was reset and recognised as belonging to the owner of the house, a Mr Jackson.

Children were often put through windows or other narrow openings to let the adult burglar in. Gipsies used children to soften up their victim, and playing on his concern for the child to cause a diversion as they picked the person's pocket.

Crimes against children

Child stripping

Some crimes were committed against children. In 1838 a group of five women stole bathing clothes from the beach at Granton. They regularly stripped children for their clothes. Working around the narrow streets at the foot of Edinburgh's Canongate the women lured well-dressed youngsters into the closes by offering them sweeties. The child's nose was covered to prevent a scream as their clothes were removed.

"It's a good shirt, Kate."
"Worth a shilling, Nell."
"Off with it!" cried Margaret Joice as they removed a bonnet, pinafore, frock, petticoats, boots and stockings from a little girl.

Curiosities of Crime in Edinburgh,
James McLevy, 1861

Four strippings in one day could bring them in a lot of money when the clothes were pawned. The child was left with only its undergarments to wander the streets until help arrived. The gang were eventually caught and each woman received eighteen months in jail.

Domestic violence

In 1868 several cases of domestic cruelty were reported. Parents often believed that they could do whatever they wanted to punish a child. Children were locked in cupboards with their hands tied behind their back, doused at wells, beaten with hairbrushes, studded belts and other objects, kicked in the face for refusing to go out and buy alcohol.

The parents were usually fined.

Children boarded out were sometimes treated harshly and had no-one to turn to. In 1944, the Royal Society for the Prevention of Cruelty to Children was alerted to a case of ill-treatment of two boys by their foster parents. The Inspector was shocked at their injuries. They had been whipped with an electric flex and the younger boy's back was completely discoloured and covered in bruises. The perpetrators were sentenced to nine and twelve months in jail.

Baby farming

On occasions parents were found guilty of murdering their children by smothering them so that they could claim insurance for the dead child which could amount to between 5/- and 25/-. They could also pawn the clothes which they received in a charity maternity bundle. Parents sometimes could not afford to feed another baby, or the child was illegitimate and an embarrassment. They would pay a woman a few pounds to take the child away. Most were then offered, for a further sum, for adoption by the 'baby farmer' who on occasions also suffocated or strangled them and received the insurance money. A small dose of laudanum was given to keep a crabbit baby quiet and often proved fatal.

Child murder

A little girl was shopping in Annan in 1868 when she was attacked, robbed, taken into a wood and murdered. Robert Smith, her attacker was seen dragging her away by a witness and was arrested. He was the last man to be publicly hanged in Dumfries in May 1868.

In the 1880s, Jessie King of Edinburgh specialised in the trade of child murder. When she could not find homes for her charges and they became a financial burden she strangled them. Two boys and a girl were murdered before she was caught. Some boys playing in the street kicked a parcel and were horrified to discover a dead baby. The others were found in boxes on waste

ground. She was executed in Edinburgh in 1889 after two attempts at suicide in the Calton Jail.

At Perth, in 1910, Robert Duff kicked his four and a half year old stepdaughter to death then tossed her body over a fence. A witness confirmed that he had kicked the child three times and the jury found him guilty. An appeal was successful in proving that his intent had not been to kill the child and he did not hang.

Juvenile crime

Reformatories

Thomas Guthrie, the pioneer of ragged schools, began to realise that a residential form of industrial school in which children who came before the courts for criminal activity could be detained would help to prevent them growing into adult criminals. There were several types of reform schools set up; the original industrial schools, farm colonies, domestic training schools and houses of refuge and training ships. Under the Dunlop Act, as the Industrial Schools Act 1854 was known, and the Young Offenders (Scotland) Act 1855 magistrates were given the power to insist on children under sixteen years of age being sent to a reformatory but they could not insist on parents ensuring their attendance. An Act of 1861 widened their powers and they could force children to remain at the school to complete their education.

In 1866, a new Act required that those found guilty of offences should board at an industrial school if the crime was considered severe enough to warrant a prison sentence. This encouraged the rapid expansion of the scheme and the 256 institutions in 1866 became 615 by 1869. Every town of note raised money by holding bazaars etc. to build its own residential industrial school, often in the big house of a country estate. It was usually described as a reformatory.

The idea was to prevent children re-offending by removing them from undesirable areas of a city and from their former companions and to make them better citizens for the future. The inmates were taught useful skills to enable them to find employment when they reached school leaving age. Under the Juvenile Delinquency Prevention and Repression Act 1878, School Boards, consisting of twelve commissioners and thirty seven directors, were set up to run these reformatories and industrial schools. There were separate Protestant and Catholic reformatories.

> *for payment to feeding schools dealing with and fitted to prevent juvenile delinquency in this city; empowered the commissioners to levy assessments of one penny per pound on the annual value of lands and heritages within the city; and to borrow in anticipation of any one year's assessment, £10,000. [1879]*
>
> The Water Supply of the City of Glasgow, J.D. Marwick, 1901

Farm Schools

The Scottish Labour Colony Association had a training farm at Kilwinning for boys in need of training and discipline. The Lads Clubs were often the receiving agents for farm trainees, who were from fourteen years of age. A representative from these would attend the Police Superintendent's Court and give advice and help to young offenders.

The Church of Scotland ran a farm school at Craigielinn, Paisley where farm work, gardening and training to be house-boys was given to boys from fourteen to eighteen years of age. They accepted boys from all denominations except Roman Catholics. All inmates agreed to attend Church of Scotland services on Sundays. Some of the boys were on probation. Another colony existed at Palacerigg, near Cumbernauld.

Marionville

By the 1860s Thomas Guthrie had bought Marionville, on the outskirts of Edinburgh. This he turned into a reformatory where 'juvenile delinquents' were taught amongst other things market gardening.

Domestic training

There were many homes for the training of girls considered to be in need of discipline run by the Social Work Committee of the Church of Scotland, the Roman Catholic Church, the Salvation Army and other organisations. Their stated aim was to place these girls in jobs, often as domestics in institutions, as not every household was prepared to take on a girl with a proven record of crimes. They took a continued interest in them and provided for their welfare.

Houses of Refuge

In Glasgow, since 1836, juvenile thieves and neglected children were placed in a House of Refuge and Reformatory for Boys. It was supported by voluntary contributions and was built close to Duke Street jail. By 1878 there were 300 incarcerated annually and it was surrounded by high walls. The building was demolished in 1925 to permit the extension of Whitehill School.

In Stranraer, in 1859, there were one hundred boys in the local reformatory. Access to alcoholic drink was blamed for many young girls offending and they were also placed in reformatories. In Aberdeen, in 1879, there were twenty five girls in residence at Mount Street. In Glasgow, in 1882, girls were moved for the second time from buildings in the city to a custom-built reformatory at East Chapelton, Bearsden. It was of elaborate Italian design and accommodated sixty girls in two dormitories. They were trained for domestic work and given schooling. In 1890 the proceeds from their industrial work brought in an income of £43.

Training Ship Movement

After the 1866 Act was passed some areas decided that the very best training which a boy could receive

Boys aboard the training ship *Cumberland,* 1869.

was a naval one. It was believed that this instilled discipline and a sense of duty in the boys as well as providing the country with seamen. The boys sent to training ships were not criminals but were wayward and had been in regular trouble with the courts. A few were boys whose parents paid to give them a first class naval training.

By 1869 two ships served the east of Scotland; at South Queensferry the *Royal Warden* housed 290 boys and the *Mars* anchored off Dundee was home to 400 between the ages of twelve and sixteen. In 1869 also an application was made to the Government for a ship to serve the west of Scotland and the *Cumberland*, a three-decked ship returned from duty in the Crimean War in poor condition, was moored on the Clyde off Helensburgh. Money was raised through bazaars to fit it out to house 350 boys aged twelve to fourteen, and staff.

Discipline was strict on all the ships. The boys were given a number. They were fed in messes, took part in watches and punishment on board was by means of the tawse or a diet of bread and water. If they were caught chewing tobacco they were made to swallow it which forced them to vomit. In 1869 fifty boys were transferred from Mossbank Reformatory to form the first group to undergo naval training aboard the *Cumberland*.

Their daily routine was to rise at 5.45am for silent prayer. They then put away their beds and blankets. They slept on straw mattresses. After washing themselves they had to scrub the decks before breakfast. Physical exercises came next followed at 9am by school. There was no break until dinner at 12.30pm. The boys took part in naval drill, rifle and cutlass practice and signalling with flags. They needed good balance to learn to climb the rigging. At 4.45pm they had tea and were then free until supper time which was at 7.30pm. By 8.30pm they had said prayers and were in bed. Relatives could visit the boys once per month.

Both schools on the *Mars* and the *Cumberland* - which never put to sea - had smaller ships attached. Some of the older boys were taken in summer on these to sail around Scotland to put their knowledge into practice. All the boys took part in sports such as gymnastics, boxing, swimming and rowing. There was also a carpenters' and tailors' workshop where boys made clothing and useful items to keep down the running cost of the ship.

Both ships had brass, flute and pipe bands which could be hired for functions and boys were eager to learn to play an instrument. The boys of the *Mars* went on holiday in summer to Elie and the locals treated them to lemonade, sweets and cakes the night before they left but the captain and officers then insisted on dosing the boys with castor-oil in case they had over-indulged. A woman was fined £5 at Leith Sheriff Court for helping boys to escape and on another occasion boys were blamed for staring a fire in the captain's quarters on the *Francis Mollison*, the tender vessel, in 1883.

The *Cumberland* was also fired and burned down in 1889. The fire started at midnight in the tailoring quarters next to the straw store. The bugler sounded the alarm and while senior boys and crew manned the pumps the ship was evacuated. Some were accommodated on the brig, *Cumbria*, some slept in the schoolhouse at Rhu while others were tendered by the *Express* to the Broomielaw where the boys were housed in the Sailors' Home.

Many of their mothers having heard rumours were waiting for them on their arrival. It was recorded that none of the boys had attempted to escape. Five boys were put on trial at Dumbarton Sheriff Court. The captain told the court that on the night of the fire the boys had been put on a diet of bread and water but had refused to take their punishment, previously they had tried to escape and were given twelve strokes of the birch. The verdict on the case was not proven.

A replacement vessel, the *Empress*, was obtained and served the movement until 1923 when it was closed down due to lack of numbers. The *Mars* was closed down in 1929 and towed away to be broken up.

Approved schools

The Young Offenders Act of 1937 changed the name from reformatory to approved school but they became known as 'bad boys homes' and just as in previous years many boys were threatened for misbehaviour with 'Ye'll get sent tae the *Mars*' so 'You'll go to the bad boys home' became the dire warning.

Courts

Children were tried in the Sheriff Court along with adults. In 1907, the Scottish Trades Union Congress agreed to a motion put forward by the Mill and Factory Workers of Brechin:

> *That this Congress is of the opinion that the prevailing practice of trying children and young persons charged with offences, in the ordinary courts, is to be deprecated, and requests the Parliamentary Committee to take steps to have a bill promoted making special children's courts obligatory - and pending this being done, instructs them to circulate authorities, requesting them to make arrangements for dealing with such cases, apart from the ordinary courts.*

> *Report of the Scottish Trades Union Congress, 1907.*

The Children's Act 1908 dealt with this problem and separate hearings were set up.

Crimes

Gambling

It was also noted that many young boys were being charged with offences related to gambling: card playing, pitch and toss and wheel of fortune. This last consisted of wooden numbers which cost a penny each. The wheel had numbered sections and was spun. When the pointer stopped at the winning number the winner received sixpence while all the rest of the money went to the showman. Three boys were fined 5/- at Wishaw in 1899 for playing pitch and toss in the square.

Vandalism

Vandalism has existed for centuries. In Dundee complaints of stone-throwing causing concern were regularly reported and in Glasgow boys indulged in stone-bickering at the Fair time between those of the north and south of the River Clyde. There were also fights with stones between the boys of the Grammar School and those of the Charity Schools in the nineteenth century. They stopped when a boy died as the result of an injury.

At Airdrie, in 1893, a boy was fined for throwing stones and breaking a window and another aged nine years of age threw a stone at an engine driver and received a fine of £1. His father was told by the Sheriff to take him home and thrash him.

> *Stone-throwing has again become rife in Hardgate. Some of the windows of the mill have been broken by malicious boys, and besides the act itself being an offence there is always the danger of persons employed in the offices and flats being injured by falling glass.*

> *In 1904 graffiti was reported as being smeared across the walls of the culvert at Boquhanran and the lights were being continually broken.*

> *Clydebank Press, 28th December, 1900*

In July 1922 several children, including one girl, broke into McAlpine's Yard, Clydebank and spilled twenty gallons of tar. They then turned the tap of an oil drum open and allowed forty gallons of oil to run out which they then set on fire.

Punishments

Prison

The Children's Act 1908 stated that young offenders must no longer be held in the same area as adult prisoners. Perth prison had a separate juvenile section but the suicide rate was extremely high.

There was no alternative to prison for children as young as five caught begging and stealing. While in prison children were often severely punished if they broke the rules. They could be handcuffed, put into a dark punishment cell, ironed - which meant having their wrists or legs attached by a chain to a bar which was attached to the walls and crossed the room horizontally.

When a young girl was sent to prison there were often lady visitors who held Bible classes and taught sewing. In 1890, those of the Catholic faith in Glasgow were visited by the Sisters of the Franciscan Convent who pleaded with them to reform. In 1901, the Glasgow Union of Women Workers organised visits to young girls in their cells and ran art and needlework classes for which rewards were given.

Minor offences

Many organisations sent representatives to attend courts and to interview boys and girls who were accused of minor offences, cautioning them against repeating the offence and offering help and advice.

Probation

In Hawick Katie Scott was appointed Police Court Sister. She visited boys and girls accused of crimes and attended court with them. In Glasgow, in 1905, a similar post was

Turnip stealing, 1930s.

created. These posts were the earliest form of what became the probation service.

In 1921, with the permission of the magistrates of Edinburgh, Katie Scott interviewed young girl offenders before they appeared in court. She collected information about the crime from the offender, teachers, the police and relatives, if there were any, and reported to the magistrate. She believed that the court should have the fullest possible information about the history, home conditions, school record and medical background of any child or young person and that proceedings on the case should be adjourned at any stage if further enquiry was considered desirable. She also made recommendations for probation.

The offender could be released under the care of a 'guardian', someone, not a probation officer, who was willing to befriend them. Girls were often placed in homes, not purely places of compulsory detention, to complete their course of work training on honour.

The Children and Young Persons (Scotland) Act 1932 permitted the juvenile courts to place offenders on a bond of good behaviour for up to three years under the supervision of a probation officer.

Birching

This was one of the punishments meted out by the Magistrates Court.

In 1900 Thomas McMillan and William Ross, both thirteen, were birched for sleeping in a yacht moored at the Forth and Clyde Canal basin, Kirkintilloch.

A boy in 1907 received ten lashes with the birch rod for stealing 2/5d from a shop till at Glasgow Road, Clydebank. Dr Dundas White, M.P. for Dumbartonshire, asked in the House of Commons, in 1909, if birching for small boys catching trout with wire snares could be abolished. A comment was made in Clydebank that there were few trout but that small boys would appreciate birching being banned for all 'crimes'. In 1917 two rivet boys received ten lashes for stealing brass nails and tools from the Naval Construction Works, Dalmuir.

Prison rhymes

There were many traditional rhymes about crime which have been handed down through the generations and are often used as skipping or ball stotting rhymes. The names of local jails are used and may be changed depending on the area.

Skitter up a lamp post
Skitter up a tree.
If you see a Polis man
Skitter in his ee.

Traditional

Goodbye Gartnavel, farewell
Barlinnie Square,
It's a long way to Milton,
but by Duke Street you'll get
there.
There's a wee convict waitin',
Wi' a big ba' an' chain,
He's been in Gartnavel fifteen
years,
noo he's oot again

Traditional

There is a happy land down in
Duke Street jail.
Where all the prisoners stand,
tied to a nail.
Bread and water for their tea,
Ham and eggs they never see
Down in that happy land, down
in Duke Street jail.

Traditional

War

near Madras in East India. Many boys became cadets as young as fourteen by lying about their age. Others went to sea as young as twelve by stowing away on cargo boats and tramp steamers to learn the ropes before joining the Navy.

Donald McInnes, in 1871, at the age of fifteen joined the Gordon Highlanders and although he was a boy soldier his duties were similar to an adult soldier's. He became a piper in the regimental band and in 1872 set sail for India. He was paid 6d per day for a seven day week and paid out 6d to a local man to do his washing. Other boys lied about their age and ran away to join the Navy.

Boer War: 1900

B for Boer, K for Kruger,
J for General French;
The British were up at the top of the hill
And the Boers were doon in the trench

Traditional

The Relief of Mafeking

The rejoicings started at 6am. Anyone going down to the yard gate at that time on Saturday morning would have been surprised to have seen thousands of workmen congregated there...It was the first time that they had heard of the long-looked for Relief of Mafeking...Pipes were speedily commandeered... flags seemed to leap from space, and in a short time all Clydebank was in a whirl of excitement as the processionists gaily marched citywards.

After breakfast the fun grew fast and furious... Works with flags, houses with flags, bairns with

flags, staid domesticated men with flags, demure young ladies with flags, coalmen with flags, hawkers with flags... The telephone men fixed a Royal Standard to the top of one of their poles. In two four-in-hand brakes, given gratis by Mr. Turnbull, apprentices paraded the Burgh led by one of them, on a charger, dressed as Baden-Powell. When Singer [sewing machine works] closed at 11 o'clock they swelled the numbers carrying in front of them an effigy of Kruger.

Clydebank Press, 5th May, 1900

World War One 1914-1918

World War One was declared against Germany in August 1914. The Territorial Army, a volunteer force, formed the basis of the Army which set off to France to win the War. Children cheered and waved flags as they gathered at railway stations and at docks to wave farewell to their fathers, uncles and older brothers. 'It'll be all over by Christmas' was the slogan. But it wasn't.

Those at home became involved in preparations for attack. There was a blackout. No lights were to be shown from windows or in the street. The idea of aeroplanes flying across the North Sea had become a possibility. As the War progressed food rationing was introduced. In 1916 ration books were seen for the first time.

Children helped to plant seed potatoes and other vegetables in plots or allotments, spare ground which was put to good use. At school

Robert Millar, aged 15, 1866.

War was something which happened at a distance and was reported in the newspapers. Professional soldiers went off to fight and that was that. Men and boys were given money - The King's Shilling - and if they took it they were legally bound to serve.

Others volunteered or were pressed, which usually meant that they were forced against their will, by the recruiting officer into service in the Navy.

Food shortages in the First World War made children realise that War did affect them and evacuation and the bombing of towns during the Second World War meant that many children were directly involved in the War.

The Services

Robert James Millar, in 1863, as a boy cadet, served in the Royal Artillery. He was a bombardier in 'E' Battery, 20th Brigade at Bangalore, girls learned to knit balaclava helmets, socks and scarves to keep the troops in the trenches warm. Children held concerts in tenement backcourts to raise money to send little extras to the fighting men. Children also helped to collect sphagnum moss which was used to dress wounds.

It was common for customers of shops to have the goods they bought, even meat and groceries, delivered to their homes by boys who rode bicycles which had baskets attached for carrying boxes. An appeal was made to customers to collect their goods if possible as there was a shortage of message boys because they were doing their bit for their country. They had left their grocer's and butcher's baskets aside to assist the Government in the munitions factories and the shipyards.

Girls from the Western Isles came to Glasgow to help in the munition works and the shipyards. Wartime creches were run by the nurses during World War One so that mothers could take part in war work but as soon as peace was declared, in most places, this facility was closed down immediately.

Cadet Corps inspection, 1914. Hutchesons' Grammar School.

Schools

Some schools, like the Royal High School, Edinburgh, set up Officer Training Corps with a grant from the Government for rifles, belts, bayonets, flags and chanters. Hutchesons' Grammar School, Glasgow, in common with other schools, set up a Cadet Corps in 1914 which attracted fifty four recruits. Boys, thirteen years of age and upwards, were accepted and by 1915 over one hundred had enrolled. They learned how to fire a musket,

semaphore and Morse signalling, went for route marches and attended a camp at Skelmorlie with the Cameronians.

Camping

For the duration of the War organisations such as the Scouts or Boys' Brigade were advised to camp indoors. Schools and church halls were used for this purpose in seaside and country areas. The Scottish Schoolboys' Club still camped out at Cademuir but no torches or camp fires were allowed.

In April 1917, the Board of Agriculture was anxious that the supply of timber should be kept up and offered to finance a camp at Murthly, if the Scottish Schoolboys' Club would provide the boys and organise their food and accommodation. Two hundred boys walked the eleven miles from Perth station to the camp. They worked from 10am - 4pm each day cutting and stacking timber. Eventually the organisation was placed in charge of six camps for eight weeks in the summer. They managed to have some fun and enjoyed sing-a-longs.

When the war is over
And the Kaiser's deid.
He's no gaun tae Heaven wi'
the eagle on his heid.
For the Lord says no!
He'll hiv tae go below,
For he's a' dressed up
An' he's got nowhere tae go.

Traditional

Victory

On the 11th November 1918 peace was declared. The Provost announced this 'joyous' news and the Town Council sent telegrams of congratulations to His Majesty King George the Fifth, Mr Lloyd-George, Prime Minister, Mr Bonar Law, General Sir Douglas Haig and Admiral Beattie.

National flags were hoisted and the streets were alive with bunting, sirens and whistles from the works hooted and crowds gathered in the streets.

Workers were dismissed for the day and everybody sang patriotic songs. The Roman Catholic Band paraded the streets of Clydebank, marching and playing as they [the crowd] went on through Dalmuir and up to Duntocher where it joined up with the Duntocher Band. The schools were closed and the children joined in the celebrations. At night there were fireworks and rockets and children improvised a band with tin cans as drums. There was only one case of drunkenness reported to the police. At Dalmuir an effigy of the Kaiser was burned on a bonfire in the park. Similar scenes took place everywhere.

Clydebank Post, 13th November, 1918

World War Two 1939 - 1945

Scotland was the first part of the United Kingdom to be bombed by enemy action. Two destroyers in the Firth of Forth were attacked on 16th October 1939 and North and South Queensferry were added to the official evacuation scheme. In June 1940 Aberdeen was the target and on 1st July at Wick two high explosive bombs were dropped killing fourteen people, seven of them children and another twenty two people were wounded. In Orkney, in 1940, there was also a fatality.

Evacuation

From 1935 the Government began to make plans against the possibility of war with Germany. One of the main provisions was a scheme to move children out of areas which they felt were likely to come under enemy attack. The only official evacuation schemes were organised in places thought most likely to be attacked: Edinburgh, Rosyth - because of the naval dockyard, - Dundee, Glasgow

Evacuees,   Cowie Collection, University of St Andrews.

and Clydebank - because of the shipbuilding yards.

Rehearsals for evacuation procedures took place months before the War started so that when war was declared on 3rd September 1939 the voluntary dispersal scheme was put into operation quickly and many mothers and children left the cities to live in the country or by the sea. Some made private arrangements with other members of their own families who lived in what were considered to be safe areas.

Children under five years of age were accompanied by their mothers but those over five went alone accompanied by teachers and members of the Women's Voluntary Service. They had no idea of where they were going or what was happening to them. Neither the children, nor anyone else, knew for how long they were being sent away from home. Some thought that it was an adventure but others were very unhappy.

The parents were informed by the school what luggage and personal items their children should take with them: warm clothes, an overcoat, a change of underclothes and stockings, night attire and a toothbrush; a tin mug, enough food

to last a day and their gas mask in its box. Many poorer parents found this a strain as they did not have spare clothing to give to their children.

The air of tinier children, the wide-eyed tots of the juvenile army, was that of a mass picnic, but the older evacuees had a quiet bearing and appeared to realise in some degree the seriousness of the situation which had created this exceptional adventure in their school experience.

At every assembly point, despite the early hour at which the first children were mustered, there was considerable bustle and liveliness. Many of the children were, of course, accompanied by their parents and guardians, in the main, their mothers. Only mothers who were voluntary helpers under the scheme or who had children under school age were permitted to travel... Large numbers of parents waited in the streets outside the assembly points while the children were given their identification labels which were attached to their clothing and had their kit inspected to see that all the essentials were there.

Besides the necessaries, small children brought favourite toys, dolls, and teddy bears, and older ones had story books and comics...milk, biscuits and bananas were uniformly distributed in all centres. As many of the children arrived as early as half-past six while the light was still grey, fathers who had not started work were also there as escorts, and in the course of the forenoon and the lunch hour, other men had come from their employment to see their children leave.

Parents who had put a brave face on the prospect of parting were obviously affected when their children went into the different railway stations...In some cases mothers broke down, and even the men were unable to disguise their momentary emotion.

The Scotsman, 2nd March, 1939

It was believed that bombing attacks would take place much earlier than they did in fact and that parents would be grateful to escape from the cities. There are many reports, however, of preparations being made for far higher numbers than those who took advantage of the scheme.

Ayr received its first contingent on Friday morning. When the first batch arrived shortly after 10.20 they were met by police under the personal supervision of Chief Constable Lowdon. The youngsters were in gay mood, many of them not having had a holiday before, and now and then amidst the buzz of conversation one could hear the 'shore' and 'sand' mentioned. Still the anxious faces of the young mothers, many carrying babies in their arms while others, obviously under school age clung to their coats, showed the grim reality of the situation. In all about 1600 children and 500 mothers came...This was much short of the number expected which was stated to be in the region of 4000.

The Ayrshire Post, 8th September, 1939

In Clydebank, in 1939, only 40% of the families eligible took part . In Glasgow, Edinburgh and Dundee, the numbers were below 50% . The same reports are available from several reception committees although it is acknowledged that some families made private arrangements with relatives.

Not everyone was happy in their new homes. There were complaints from those who were used to having shops below their tenement houses and a cinema just along the road that the country was too quiet. Many returned home immediately to be followed, when the expected raids did not take place, by many more. In Clydebank (which was devastated by German bombers in March 1941) around 75% of those evacuated were estimated to have returned within the first year.

Several families who were taken to places on the outskirts of Ayr are reported to have gone home on Friday night stating that it was too lonely for them.

The Ayrshire Post, 8th September, 1939

DIDN'T LIKE VILLAGE LIFE

Seven boys of about eleven years of age arrived at Ballantrae from Glasgow on Friday as part of the city evacuation scheme. They had a wash and food at the house which was to be their billeting quarters and later had a walk round the village. Finding village life rather irksome after the busy streets of Glasgow the boys set off on foot for Girvan twelve miles away. They were found at Girvan by the police and taken to the police station where the 'evacuees' were lodged for the night. On Saturday a private car arrived for the 'escaped' boys and they were taken back to their billets.

The Ayrshire Post, 8th September, 1939

Reception areas

Carrier bags were being industriously filled with tins of corned beef and milk and packets of chocolate to be ready for distribution. The Women's Voluntary Services had been collecting bedding and crockery and serving them out to householders to augment their supplies. Farm workers were perspiring as they made up palliasses [hessian sacks filled with straw to act as mattresses]. Active helpers were making halls ready for the visitors, collecting food and preparing tea to be served on the arrival of the evacuees.

Evacuation in Scotland, William Boyd, 1944

Many children were taken on long journeys in poorly lit trains without corridors which meant that there were no toilet facilities. Even in corridor trains there was little comfort as they were so crowded and the food and drink were inadequate for the length of the journey. Some children were taken as far north from Glasgow as Aberdeen and they arrived dirty, tired and hungry. One train had been delayed in sidings for long periods at a time and the journey had taken over twelve hours. Perth, Wigtown and Kintyre also felt that despite rehearsals the operation was a shambles.

Many mothers and children sent to Banchory wanted to go home to Dundee within twenty four hours complaining that, 'They country folk a' live on parritch, bread and butter' or 'I'm that feart o' coos'.

Vermin

At Crieff there were several complaints that the children arrived with verminous bodies and hair and that some even had infectious diseases. The children should have been inspected for lice, vermin or infectious disease before travelling but this had not always been carried out. In many areas complaints were received by the billeting officers of children having scabies, a skin disease. Others had whooping cough and, a few, German measles. Some householders demanded that the child be immediately sent to hospital. The receiving authorities felt that this lack of assurance that all children would be medically cleared made a mockery of their promises to the people who were offering shelter in their homes and would make it even more difficult for future intakes.

Blitz

After the blitz on Clydebank on 13th and 14th March 1941 and the bombing of the Clyde Estuary, Greenock, Port Glasgow and Dumbarton were added to the evacuation scheme. Many people were left homeless and had to be evacuated elsewhere. Schools, as well as other public buildings, were used as rest centres.

14/3/41

At 12.45pm Headmaster received phone message to be ready to receive 800 evacuees for tea. All staff volunteered to remain behind and assist. Later the number was changed to 450 who were to be fed and sleep here until billeting was completed.

At 8.40 the first lot arrived. They were sent to the dining hall where they received a substantial meal. Bus loads came in succession until the assembly hall was packed with men, women, children, babies and some dogs. Many had cases, others had nothing but their working clothes on, women in house slippers etc..

15/3/41 All evacuees were fed breakfast, dinner and tea. Room 1 became a billeting centre from which people were sent in army lorries to houses in the town.

16/3/41 Same as yesterday.

17 & 18 Numbers fell as people were billeted. School closed for a week owing to it being used as a rest centre.

24/3/41 School reopened today after being closed since 14th March.

Enrolled 93 evacuees from Clydebank and Glasgow R.C. schools.

The History of St Ninian's High School, Kirkintilloch, 1960

Billeting

This was the name given to the placing of families with householders in safe areas. Everyone had to register the number of empty rooms in their home. A billeting officer then assigned the number of children or a family to that house. Not everyone was happy. Both the owner of the house and those who had to live there were upset by having to share cooking and toilet facilities with strangers.

The Billetee

The poets praise the cuckoo -
I call it silly gush,
Why don't they try to visualise
the viewpoint of the thrush?
It's easy for the poet
To praise this springtime guest:
He would not sing as much if
he'd
A cuckoo in his nest.
His song of careless rapture
Would take a minor key
If he went home one day and
found
He'd gained a billetee.

St Andrews Citizen, 28th September, 1947

Large houses were commandeered and it wasn't only children who were evacuated but entire schools were sent off to live and work in large houses in the countryside. In 1941, sixty seven Hutchesons' Girls' Grammar School pupils and seven staff were evacuated to Dalry, Kircudbrightshire. As reported in the *Scottish Field* in March 1944, they helped the local war effort by knitting woolly toys for the Red Cross shop in Castle Douglas and worked for three week spells as land girls on local farms.

Hiawatha in the Stewartry (1941 - 1944)

From Whitehall came forth the
edict:
"Let there be evacuation,
Let the maids of Hutchy
Grammar
Now proceed into the Stewartry.
Let them occupy the mansion
Now vacated by Lord Sinclair".

Hutchesons' Girls' Grammar School Anniversary Magazine, 1876 - 1946

Immigrants

Another aspect of evacuation was the number of children who were billeted in Scotland from the areas of England which came under heavy air attack from the German bombers: Birmingham, Manchester, Coventry and London. There were also many children from the Channel Islands which were occupied by German forces, and even children from Germany, the Kinderfolk, who had escaped from Nazi rule. Many are still living in Scotland today.

A boy came into our class. His real name was French and was difficult to pronounce so we called him Harry Paterson. He had been evacuated from Guernsey and came to live with the Patersons across the road from us. They were a very old couple with two unmarried daughters who were old as well. He was taller than most of the other boys in our class. I think that he might have been older than us. He was all right. He soon learned to play kick the can and A leavy O up by the garages.

Douglas Middleton, aged 7, 1944

Camps

The Scottish Special Housing Association set up camps for evacuees, in 1939, at Meigle. There were complaints of malicious damage being done by the children.

Emigration

Some parents felt that their children would be safe if they were sent abroad to South Africa or Canada. Under a Government sponsored evacuation scheme many set sail on the *Arandora Star*, and the *Volendam*, a ship of a Dutch line. Both ships were torpedoed, the *Arandora* on 2nd July and the *Volendam* on 30th August 1940, and sunk, although some children did survive and reached the Clyde. A nine year old Dundee girl, Sheila Carswell, survived. Her only complaint was that she didn't like the dry ship's biscuits served on the lifeboat.

Many children set out again on the *City of Benares*, sailing this time from Liverpool with the assurance that the ship would have a convoy. This proved inadequate, however, and the German submarine found its target. A report sent to the Commander-in-Chief by the rescue vessel, HMS *Hurricane*, on 18th September 1940 stated 'There are no other survivors' after only 102 of the 406 on board were accounted for. However, one lifeboat reported capsized did escape and after eight days tossing in the Atlantic and after two false alarms, when ships which they thought had seen them sailed away, forty six survivors were rescued by a Sunderland bomber and the destroyer HMS *Anthony* and eventually docked at Gourock.

After being landed at Gourock the six boys, Mary Cornish, a teacher, were feted as heroes. Father O'Sullivan, still a sick man, was shown his obituary notice and thought it was "quite nicely written".

The Sunday Express, 5th May, 1900

Girls' Training Corps, 1942.
Hutchesons' Grammar School.

Youth Organisations

Girls' Training Corps

In June 1942 Hutchesons' Girls' Grammar School set up a Girls' Training Corps. Drill parades took place on Friday afternoons. They learned first-aid and also gave help with their children and chores to mothers whose husbands were in the Services. Even in their adopted home, after evacuation to Dalry, Kircudbright, they set up a Junior GTC jointly with local girls.

Boy Scouts and Boys' Brigade

Mobilisation

In this time of National Emergency comes the opportunity for the Scouts' Organisation to show it can be of material service to the country. Just as the boys at Mafeking were utilised to take the lighter work of men in order that these may be released to the more arduous duties of war, so can the Scouts give valuable assistance to the State at home.

Robert Baden-Powell, 1939

Throughout Scotland Boy Scout Troops and Boys' Brigade Companies were asked to help to prepare sandbags for piling against buildings as a protection against bomb attacks. On a Saturday morning and on weekday evenings they filled hundreds of canvas bags with one cwt. of sand. In 1939 they also helped to distribute gasmasks to every home.

Spies

The Scouts also had the job of guarding and patrolling bridges, culverts and telephone lines against sabotage by spies.

Alex Becket and Arthur Blair were patrolling on the evening of Tuesday 18th August at Milngavie Waterworks, access to which was closed to the public. Alex spotted a man coming over the wall from Strathblane Road. The man had not gone far when Scout Becket stopped him and asked him to show his permit. This he was not able to do, nor would he give information about himself... The Scout asked the man to write down his name

and he noticed the German script of the letter 'B'. Scout Blair arrived on the scene and waterworks staff were alerted. The man, a schoolmaster - Herr L. Buhring - fluent in English, was taken off to Maryhill Barracks.

Milngavie Advertiser, 20th August, 1940

Messengers

During air-raid warnings members of both organisations ran on foot or cycled between ARP posts with information.

When the sirens sounded at Partick, on the evening of the 13th March 1941, Neil Leitch, who was sixteen, jumped onto his bicycle to report to the local fire station. He was sent to Hyndland with a fire officer. As the raids began he set off back to Partick with a message and fell off his cycle several times as it was shaken by blasts. After receiving first-aid he set out again despite warnings and arrived at Partick Fire Station as it received a direct hit from a high explosive bomb. He was badly injured and later died. The Lord Provost of Glasgow, Sir Patrick Dollan, and the members of the fire brigade honoured his memory by placing a Celtic Cross over his grave in Dalbeth Cemetery.

Adapted from, *Firemen at War 1939 - 1945*, 1947-48

National Service Badge

This was a red badge which was worn above the right shirt pocket of the Scouts uniform to show that service had been carried out. A similar honour was worn by members of the Boys' Brigade.

School parties and timber camps

Fifth and sixth year pupils in schools in Scotland were encouraged to undertake service to the community during the summer holidays. Forestry was popular and senior pupils from

At Dundee a special Police Auxiliary Messenger Service was organised. There were fifty two boys recruited to carry messages around the town. © D.C. Thomson & Co Ltd.

Whitehill School, Glasgow, like many other school parties, took off in the summer holidays in the 1940s. They lived in hutted accommodation at Kilmun on the Firth of Clyde where they helped to fell branches of trees and cut them up for logs. The highlight of one 'camp' was the return to the Holy Loch of a submarine depot ship from Canada with white bread and strawberry jam aboard making a welcome change from mock chocolate spread and syrup sandwiches which had been the only fillings available.

Berry picking

Raspberries and other soft fruit was grown in Perthshire, especially around Blairgowrie, and berrypickers were needed to pick the fruit by hand. With men and women away at war schoolchildren camped in the area and helped with the fruit harvest.

Salvage and savings

Everything which could be re-used in one form or another was saved. 'Waste not! Want not!' was the slogan. The uniformed organisations were heavily involved in collecting waste paper, bones and metal which they took to the depots, often run by the Women's Voluntary Service, from where it was sent off to be recycled. Boys and girls went around with trek carts collecting bundles of waste. Special waste drives were held and people were continually encouraged to reach a higher target. These achievements were published in local papers and citizens were proud if their area was near the top of the list.

Girl Guides, Scouts and Boys' Brigade, in Clydebank, in October 1940 collected:

76 tons of paper and cardboard
30 tons of scrap metal
1 ton of non-ferrous metal
3 tons of rags

Children filling sandbags.
Cowie Collection, University of St Andrews.

National Book Recovery Drive

This took place throughout Scotland in April 1943. Books and periodicals were collected which were suitable to be sent to the H.M. Forces. Rare or technical books were given to libraries and other books were pulped to make paper for maps etc. The Ministry of Supply organised the scheme through local authorities and the youth organisations played their part.

Make-do-and-mend

This was a slogan aimed at the repair and re-use of material for clothing. When a child grew out of a dress if it was a plain material pieces of a contrasting colour or patterned print would be inserted into the bodice and skirt to make it wider and longer.

If it was originally a printed fabric then plain inserts gave it a new lease of life. Boys had leather patches sewn onto the elbows of jerseys and jackets and sometimes around the edge of the cuffs. Woollen blankets were dyed and made into coats and

siren suits. Adult clothing was made down to fit children. Those lucky enough to have relations in Canada, Australia or South Africa were sent parcels of cast-offs which were gratefully received.

I remember that in 1942, when I was five, one of my aunts was being married to a soldier. I couldn't believe my luck when this fantastic pale pink organdie dress arrived from Canada. Although I was not normally a frilly child I felt like a princess in it. My mother was delighted to be given a pair of silver party

Dundee Scouts collecting salvage.
© D.C. Thomson & Co Ltd.

shoes, several pairs of which had been found in boxes in the basement of James Allan's, the shoe shop, by one of our neighbours who worked there. When asked where on earth I had got such a prized possession I am said to have replied, "It's a secret and I'm not allowed to tell you."

Interview with Sheila Peters, 1997

Wings for Victory, Spitfire Funds, Dig for Victory, War Weapons Weeks, Warship Week, Salute the Soldier and Ship Halfpennies saved to buy

books for sailors through the British Sailor's Society were all campaigns in which children played their part.

Registration

The head of every household had to fill in a form on Friday 20th September 1939 giving particulars of every person staying in the house on that night. From this information a National Register was compiled.

Identity cards

Identity cards were issued which showed the owner's name, the district in which they lived and a serial number which indicated the position of that person in the household. This was used for registering for ration books and clothing coupons.

Identity disks

These were disks made of cardboard or in some cases of bone with a hole in them through which a ribbon was threaded in a loop. This was worn around the child's neck. On one side there was the name and address of the child and on the other the name or names and addresses of nearby relatives. This was in case of emergency, or if anything happened to the child during an air raid and the parents could not be traced then the next of kin would be informed.

Air-raid precautions

All children were issued with gasmasks as there was a fear that poison gas would be used by the

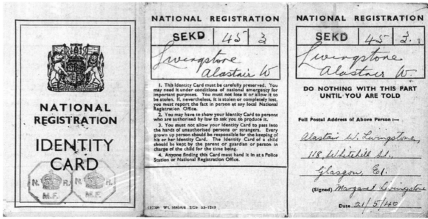

ID card, Alastair Livingstone.

enemy. Some were specially designed for babies. Children under five had pink rubber Mickey Mouse ones and those over five were given black ones just like adults. The masks were made of rubber and fastened behind the head with straps. There was a perspex window to see through. There was a metal mouthpiece with tiny holes to let you breath. This was filled with charcoal which absorbed gases and had a filter inside to prevent gas passing through.

Gas mask drill

Whenever a child went out the gas mask had to be carried. It was kept in a square carrying-case of cardboard, canvas or leather with a strap to put over the shoulder. At school gas mask drills were regularly called. When the bell rang each class had to file out and assemble ready to go to the air-raid shelter. Names were checked and masks were put on as quickly as possible.

cosy in an emergency

Girls' Shop:
Fourth Floor.

The "On Guard" Siren Suit.

Anderson shelter grassed over.

Air-raid shelters

Brick shelters were put up in school playgrounds for the use of the public as well as the pupils. People had Morrison shelters, a sort of cage which was put up in the living-room or Anderson shelters which were built in gardens, partly sunk into the ground. They were made of corrugated sheets and covered with turf.

I loved playing on top of our Anderson shelter. We pretended that it was a mountain. The night of the Clydebank Blitz, in March 1941 when I was four, I remember being lifted out of bed and dressed in my siren suit which was made of warm brown material. My Mum called it my teddy-bear outfit. My cousins, Robin and Iain Strain from Kirkcaldy were staying with us that night, my Aunt Ruby and my grandmother were there also.

The sky was crissed-crossed with beams of light from the searchlights and the ack-ack guns were firing from the battery up on the hill. There was an orange light in the distance which must have been the fires at Maryhill and Clydebank. We huddled into the Anderson shelter. It had wooden benches. The two small ones, like bunks,

across the back were where we children were put to bed. The door had a wire mesh cover, a wooden insert with holes the size of an old penny, probably to let air in, and another mesh on the outside. The shelter smelled of damp earth, like the smell in an underground train station. There was a big black metal box with a hinged lid and a handle, it might have once been a coal scuttle, filled with tinned food. These were our emergency rations.

Interview with Sheila Peters, 1997

Blitz

In the park hundreds of women and children waited patiently for something to happen, bombed out, dazed, homeless...one little girl stood in front of the town hall dressed in a spotless skating outfit clutching her white kid skating boots.

Evening Citizen, 11th March, 1955

I saw lorries driving away from St James' Parish Church and I asked my mother "What is under the tarpaulins?" She said, "Bodies taken from the Holy City."

Oral history archive, Dalmuir Educational Resource Centre, 1982

My mother carried a small box of belongings - insurance policies and such things - she told me to stay in bed while she went outside for a breath of fresh air - that was the last I saw of her.

Oral history archive, Dalmuir Educational Resource Centre, 1982

Accidents

Young Evacuees Lose Lives

Two little Glasgow children - evacuated a fortnight ago - were drowned yesterday by the incoming Solway tide. An eleven year old girl, a playmate of the children made a heroic but unsuccessful effort to save her friends.

The victims of the tragedy are Betty Brennan (9) and her little brother Eric Brennan (7). The children along with the remainder of the family, Sarah (11) and Raymond (2), left home at 294, Tollcross Road, Glasgow, with their mother a week on Sunday last.

The four children have lived at Gretna with their mother since and they were playing together when the tragedy occurred. With them was a Glasgow family named Brogan, of 161 Tollcross Road. Along with playmates, Ann, Jean and Margaret Brogan aged 10, 8 and 11 respectively, Betty Brennan was playing on a pipe-line on the sands. Her brother, Eric was on one of the supports of the pipe, slightly lower than his sister. As the tide came in, he failed to climb back on to the pipe and as the water reached his legs Betty reached down and gripped him...

'We were playing on the pipe [said Margaret Brogan] when the tide began to come in. Eric was farthest out below the pipe. I went to him and then there was Betty. Eric began to cry as the water came over his feet. Betty took hold of his hand and I, in turn, caught hold of Betty's. Eric

lost his balance and fell in the water, and we pulled to try and get him up. However, Betty fell in too and as I was in danger of being dragged in too I had to let go. I saw a log of wood and I shouted "Betty, Betty, try to get this," but she was carried away by the tide and I never saw her again.'

Daily Record, 14th September, 1939

News

Children listened to the wireless, as radio was called, and saw reports on *Pathe News* at the cinema. At school a war diary had to be kept but it was often puzzling and difficult for children to understand why anyone would want to kill them by dropping bombs from an aeroplane.

"Have you heard the news? Great news! Wonderful news!" It was 6th June 1944 - D-Day. We weren't quite sure what was happening...adults were glued to the wireless... later, however we were able to revel in the newsreel reports at the picture house...so action-packed that they even surpassed the adventures of our cowboy hero, Roy Rodgers, and his horse Trigger.

Auchinairn and Bishopbriggs at War,
Bill Findlay, 1995

Children began to hope that at last their fathers would be coming home but it was not until May 1945 that V.E.Day (Victory in Europe) was celebrated and World War Two did not end until the Japanese surrender on 14th August 1945.

V.E. Day

There were brass and pipe bands in the streets. Impromptu processions formed, waving flags and dancing and singing broke out. Bonfires sprang up all over the place and effigies of Adolf Hitler were burnt.

Clydebank and district is a little breathless this weekend after its large-scale celebrations on Victory in Europe Day and V E Plus One...Shopkeepers and householders at the weekend began to display flags, bunting and streamers, and by Monday afternoon the decorations increased so that by the evening all was in readiness for the long-awaited news...Coloured fairy-lights also outlined the Municipal Buildings...Children went wild with excitement at, for many, their first glimpse of illumin-ations, and danced and shouted.

Clydebank Press, 11th May, 1945

Thank you, Foster-Parents . . . we want more like you!

Thank you, Mrs. Evans . . . we want more like you!

WAR: THE HUMANITIES CURRICULUM PROJECT
© SCHOOLS COUNCIL PUBLICATIONS
Published by Heinemann Educational Books, 48 Charles Street, London WIX 8AH

Acknowledgements:

E. Bushnell, Archivist,
    St Leonard's School, St Andrews
Ron Caird, D. C. Thomson & Co. Ltd.
Audrey Canning, Librarian, S.T.U.C.
Don Martin, East Dunbartonshire Libraries
Brian Osborne, Scottish Library Association
Alastair Ramage,
    Heatherbank Museum of Social Work
Alan Reid, S.L.A. Publications Officer
D. R. Ward, Rector, Hutchesons' Grammar School
Bell Library, Perth
Dundee Central Library
Edinburgh Central Library
Scottish Schoolboys' Club
Jim Barr, Margaret Borland, David Conchie, Ruth Currie, Bob Dawson, Bill Findlay, Sheila Lewis, Minna Taylor.

Places to visit

Museum of Childhood, Edinburgh
Highland Museum of Childhood, Strathpeffer
Toy Museum, Isle of Skye

Further Reading:

Auchenairn and Bishopbriggs at War, W. Findlay,
    Strathkelvin District Libraries, 1995
Children of the State, F. Davenport-Hill and
    F. Fowke, Macmillan, 1889
The Dawn of Scottish Social Welfare,
    Thomas Ferguson, Thomas Nelson, 1948
Empty Cradles, Margaret Humphries,
    Child Migrant Trust, 1995
The Good Morning School, Lileen Hardy,
    Gay and Hancock, 1912
The Health of Glasgow, A. K. Chalmers, 1930
The Life Story of William Quarrier, J. Urquhart, 1900
Seedtime and Harvest of Ragged Schools,
    Thomas Guthrie, A & C Black, 1860
Good Words
Poor Law Magazine and Parochial Journal
Annual reports, newspapers, etc.

Front cover: Children at St Leonard's Seniors' Convalescent Home, St Andrews, 1903.

St. Leonard's School for Girls Archive.

Inside front cover: Montage of children taking part in celebrations.

Back cover: Washing at the Tenement Kitchen Sink, A. C. Lillie, Springburn Museum.

Inside back cover: Children taking part in the Rent Strike, 1917, West Dunbartonshire Libraries.

Index

Money conversion table

1/-	=	5p
2/-	=	10p
5/-	=	25p
10/-	=	50p
30/-	=	£1.50